NATED BY ME ON THE _12_ DAY OF ? May

Birthplace	Citizen	Mother tongue	Occupation					Education		Ownership			
quina		English	Farmer	General Farm Emp				yes yes		O M F 177			
mississippi		English	Farmer	General Farm O A				Yes yes		R F			
mississippi		English	Farmer	General Farm O A				Yes yes		R F			
mississippi		English	Farm laborer	Home Farm	W	No	0	yes yes yes					
mississippi		English	Farm Laborer	Home Farm	W	No	0	yes yes yes					
mississippi		English	Farm Laborer	Home Farm	W	No	0	yes yes yes					
mississippi			None										
mississippi		English	Farm Laborer	Home Farm	W	No	0	yes yes yes					
ed States		English	Farmer	General Farm Emp				yes yes		O M F 162			
orgia		English	None					yes yes					
mississippi		English	Farm Laborer	Home Farm	W	No	0	yes yes No					
mississippi		English	Farm Laborer	Home Farm	W	No	0	yes yes yes					
mississippi		English	Farm Laborer	Home Farm	W	No	0	yes yes yes					
mississippi		English	Farm Laborer	Home Farm	W	No	0	yes yes yes					
mississippi			None										
mississippi			None										
mississippi			None										
mississippi			None										
th Carolina		English	Farmer	General Farm Emp				yes yes		O F F 193			
Carolina		English	Farm Laborer	Home Farm	W	No	0	No No					
th Carolina		English	Farmer	General Farm Emp				yes yes		R F 190			
mississippi		English	Farm Laborer	Home Farm	W	No	0	yes yes yes					
mississippi		English	Farm Laborer	Home Farm	W	No	0	yes yes yes					
mississippi		English	Farm Laborer	Home Farm	W	No	0	yes yes yes					
mississippi		English	Farm Laborer	Home Farm	W	No	0	yes yes yes					
mississippi			None										
Carolina		English	Farmer	General Farm Emp				yes yes		O F F 190			
mississippi		English	Farm Laborer	Home Farm	W	No	0	yes yes yes					
mississippi		English	Farm Laborer	Home Farm	W	No	0	yes yes yes					
mississippi		English	Farm Laborer	Home Farm	W	No	0	yes yes yes					
mississippi			Farm Laborer	Home Farm	W	No	0	No					
mississippi			Farm Laborer	Home Farm	W	No	0						
mississippi			None					No					
mississippi			None					No					
mississippi			None					No					
mississippi		English	Farmer	General Farm Emp				yes No		R F 166			
mississippi		English	Farm Laborer	Home Farm	W	No	0	No No					
mississippi			None					No					
mississippi			None					No					
mississippi			None										
Carolina		English	Farmer	General Farm O A				yes yes		R F 178			
gia		English	None					yes yes					
Carolina		English	Farmer	General ? O A				yes yes		O M F 166			
mississippi		English	None					yes yes No					
mississippi			None										
mississippi			None										
mississippi		English	Farmer	General Farm Emp				yes yes		R F 189			
mississippi		English	None					No No					
mississippi		English	Farm Laborer	Home Farm	W	No	0	yes No yes					

FINDING *Oprah's* ROOTS

FINDING

Oprah's
ROOTS

FINDING YOUR OWN

HENRY LOUIS GATES, JR.

CROWN PUBLISHERS
NEW YORK

Copyright © 2007 by Henry Louis Gates, Jr.

Published in the United States by Crown Publishers, an imprint of the Crown Publishing Group,
a division of Random House, Inc., New York.

www.crownpublishing.com

Crown is a trademark and the Crown colophon is a registered trademark of Random House, Inc.

Library of Congress Cataloging-in-Publication Data

Gates, Henry Louis.
Finding Oprah's roots : finding your own / Henry Louis Gates, Jr.—1st ed.
1. African Americans—Genealogy—Handbooks, manuals, etc. I. Title.
E185.96.G383 2007
929'.1072—dc22   2006036059

ISBN 978-0-307-38238-2

Printed in the U.S.A.

Design by Lenny Henderson

10 9 8 7 6 5 4 3 2 1

First Edition

For Henry Finder

Contents

"If a race has no history, if it has no worthwhile tradition, it becomes a negligible factor in the thought of the world, and it stands in danger of being exterminated."

—CARTER G. WOODSON

"What was your name? And why don't you now know what your name was then? Where did it go? Where did you lose it? Who took it? And how did he take it?"

—MALCOLM X

Introduction

his is a book about finding your roots—how one goes about the intriguing, fascinating, sometimes frustrating process of determining the identity of the many individuals who make up the many branches of your family tree.

Genealogical research today combines detective work, history, and science in a way that can be intensely thrilling, regardless of who you are or where your ancestors came from, whether Western Europe, the Middle East, the Far East, Latin America, or Africa. Judging from the range of emotions that experiencing this process released in me, I believe that recovering the ancestors on one's family tree can be especially rewarding for African Americans, in part because of the tragedy of our shared history as the descendants of slaves, people whose identity has been largely invisible to us. Of course, it can also be a very difficult undertaking, one that requires many painstaking hours and the patience to endure many false leads.

For an African American, tracing one's ancestors can also be a very painful experience: When one is fortunate enough to discover the identity of an ancestor who lived as a slave, one is forced to relive the brutal details of the slave past, a past that our ancestors experienced not in the abstract, of course, as we do through history books or films, but in their everyday lives. Discovering the identities of one's ancestors who lived through, and survived, the horrors of the "peculiar institution" of slavery makes American history, generally, and

African American history, more specifically, tangible and immediate and palpable, in a manner not otherwise experienced. Genealogy can be a veritable time machine, enabling us all, to some extent, to be travelers through time and space, reencountering the past in the most particular or personal way. For African Americans, whose access to their collective historical past has been severely limited until very recently, genealogy can open a window or portal onto the broad past of their people since they arrived on these shores as slaves precisely by resurrecting the identities of their own direct ancestors.

In writing this book, I've tried to be open and honest about what we can and cannot do through genealogy. I want to share with you the steps you must take to unearth your family's past, even though I know that not all of your efforts will bear fruit. Nevertheless, from my own experience, I know that the end result will be well worthwhile, even when one's searches inevitably meet with dead ends.

I've decided to focus this book on examples drawn from the PBS documentary *Oprah's Roots,* which aired in January 2007. I was the executive producer of that documentary, as well as its on-camera host. Based on her experience with the program, Oprah Winfrey has generously agreed to allow me to use details we uncovered while researching her family tree so that you'll have a sense of what is involved in the genealogical research process. I expect that these examples will also prove entertaining—primarily because Oprah has an especially fascinating family tree. Using a mix of old-fashioned sleuthing and the most sophisticated techniques of modern genealogical analysis, we were able to trace her roots back to the early part of the nineteenth century, when her great-great-grandparents were slaves in Mississippi. Then, with state-of-the-art DNA analysis, we were able to go back even further, all the way to Africa.

If we could find out so much detail about Oprah Winfrey's ancestors, we most certainly can help you to find out a great deal about yours. Indeed, the evidence is already out there: in original documents now digitized and available through the Internet as well as those still buried in dusty archives. You just need to know where to look for it—and what to look for. I'm going to try to supply you with that information.

To undertake the research for this project, I was very fortunate to be able to employ three absolutely top-notch genealogists, Jane Ailes, Johni Cerny, and Jan Hillegas. They did an incredible job—digging around in libraries and attics and churches all over the country, even visiting some old graveyards. Their efforts yielded invaluable results: They discovered information about Oprah's ancestors that researchers had been looking for for more than twenty years! And they shared their knowledge of the genealogical research process with me, which was a revelatory experience. I am a trained scholar. I know how to look for old documents, how to decode their sometimes Byzantine meanings, how to interpret and understand the past, but there were many things I needed to learn about building a family tree. There are many tricks to that endlessly fascinating trade.

Although I was lucky that I could work with professional genealogists with years of accrued wisdom, you may not be so fortunate. That is why I decided to write this book: to share their research methods with you as best I can. I sincerely believe that if you're willing to put in the work, you can use these techniques to identify your ancestors, even if those ancestors were nameless, illiterate slaves, not even recognized in their lifetimes as human beings, with legitimate names, by the larger American society.

Why do this? I mean, it is perfectly irrelevant, in one sense, what one's ancestors did a century or two ago. The fact that my great-great-great-great-grandfather was an excellent casket-maker has no bearing on my life, at least none that I can perceive immediately. But, of course, that's not the point. Understanding our history, as Americans and as African Americans, can sometimes help us to imagine our future—our future as individuals, our future as a people. The great African American historian Carter G. Woodson famously wrote that a people cannot determine their future adequately if they're ignorant of their past. For Woodson, this aphorism was a call to arms for black people to record and write and study their own history as if their lives—or the collective life of our people—depended upon creating a written historical record. But this is as true for individuals and families as it is for an entire ethnic group; in fact, I believe that reconstructing their family's past with as much specificity as the historical archives will allow is an even more urgent task for individuals—especially African American individuals and their families. Doing so enables us all to begin to tell a new narrative of American history as a whole, and helps us to understand new dimensions about our individual selves, about how we got here from there, how we emerged as the person we are from a long line of sometimes quirky, sometimes cantankerous ancestors, our direct genealogical kinsmen and women.

On a grand scale, reconstructing our individual family's past, finding all of its branches and confronting all of its complexities, piece by piece, bit by bit, is the only way to begin to re-create, to retell, the larger narrative of American history. After all, a people's historical narrative can consist only of a summary of the voices that created that history. And if our voices have been silenced or excluded, how can the black voice testify to what we have done, what we have seen, what we have heard since our ancestors first landed in this country in the early 1600s? How else can we testify to how we got over the thicket and morass of slavery, Jim Crow segregation, the war for our civil rights, and beyond? Embracing our individual histories enables us to expand the collective narrative of America, helping all of us to understand that the founding of this republic was not only red, white, and blue, it was also, indelibly, black.

But I believe that telling our family's stories, reconstructing our family trees, contributes to the development of American society in another manner, one just as profound if not as grand. And that result is achieved by a curious process of what I think of as "anchoring," or "grounding," a process that can arise from the intimacy of familiarity with one's own people's past. We are grounded by knowing where our grandparents lived, what they did, and from where their own grandparents came. We are grounded by knowing the past well enough to connect it to our lives today. And this process confers a certain peculiar sense of pride that cannot be obtained by other means, especially for those of us previously denied access to our family's history. And this is as true for members of other ethnic groups as it is for African Americans.

The concept of the past, of course, has many levels—especially today, as human beings have become fascinated with the science of DNA analysis. We are now willing and able to test exhaustively our genetic makeup in an attempt to learn something about our ancestral past in a way that was virtually impossible just one generation ago. Am I Irish, or Jewish, or Polish, or Chinese? Do I share any genetic markers with Native Americans? Are my recent ancestors from Africa? And I say "recent" because all of us, we now know, are descended—through tens of thousands of years—from human beings who originated in Africa. If so, what "tribe" am I from? Am I Yoruba, or Asante, Kpelle, or Zulu? Can DNA yield such specific results? Despite the fact that this sort of ancestry-tracing is destined to remain anonymous—that is, destined not to yield the names of any of the individuals on our distant family trees—millions of Americans are paying to receive kits through the mail that instruct them to swab the inside of their cheeks to learn more about their most remote ancestors. Learning these results can be enormously satisfying; I know it has been for me.

At the same time, supplementing or paralleling this sort of broad, or anonymous, analysis with genealogical research—by recording the names and, sometimes, even painting the faces of our more recent ancestors on our family trees—can be equally exciting. Indeed, as I learned from Oprah, it can be even more exhilarating and satisfying to learn the identities of our great-great-grandparents and to encounter some of the details of their lives, than it is to learn more abstract facts about ancestors who lived thousands of years ago—ancestors whose names we can never possibly know.

Both processes, however—the genetic and the genealogical—can combine to give each of us a sense of place, a sense of rooted-ness, within that grand sweep of evolution that is our common history as human beings, helping us to understand, at long last, from which particular little branch or twig of the forest of human development we've descended. Who were "my" people? Do I look like them? Am I "like" them in some fundamental way? Do I share characteristics of my personality with them? Am I the way I am because of some shared tic or tendency that has been passed down through our shared family environment, the environmental equivalent, if such a thing exists, of mother's milk?

The last diary entry that Frederick Douglass was to make, shortly before he died, was this: "Still no evidence of my birth date." It was 1894, Frederick Douglass was the most famous black man in history, and to his dying day in 1895, the one question that haunted him was "When was I born?" It is the ultimate question of the rootless, followed closely by "What is my name?"—meaning who, precisely, were my individual ancestors? And Douglass passed away without ever possessing the answer to the question of his birth date, or to the question of his father's identity. In fact, he cited this—of all things—as the single most significant difference between a slave and a free person, indeed, between a black person and a white person: the knowledge of one's birth date, the ownership of time through mastery of the calendar, and, of course, the literacy to record the date that the calendar signifies on the day of one's birth. Dickson J. Preston, an historian, would later ascertain Douglass's birth date, but Douglass himself never could. And, in a very real sense, that knowledge—the knowledge of linear time and how to record it, the knowledge of one's name along with one's birth date, and the capacity to write down both—is the hidden secret of the whole of African American history. It is a secret that haunts us, even today, as so many of our children are functionally illiterate, barely able to spell or write their names, let alone read with comprehension the front page of a newspaper. Far too many of us have forgotten that the "blackest" part of the black tradition was mastering the fine arts of reading and writing, even—no, especially—when racists made laws making literacy-training illegal for black people.

We cannot afford to keep this secret hidden much longer. If we want to go forward as a people, we need to be able to look back and discover where we came from. We need to get ourselves grounded, and the process starts by grounding ourselves in our own family's extended past. I hope that this book will inspire you with the stories we uncovered that connect Oprah Gail Winfrey to the several branches that comprise her family's fascinating lineage. Then, if you wish, it may help you do the same for yourself, by enabling you to feel the inimitable sense of connection, of belonging—indeed, the sense of grasping your own "roots," as Alex Haley famously put it— that can be found only by unearthing the roots and branches of your own historically unique family tree.

Henry Louis Gates, Jr.
Cambridge, Massachusetts
September 30, 2006

PART ONE

Beginnings

*H*ave you ever been to Ellis Island? It is a remarkably moving tourist site, the repository of so very many historical memories. But when I observed the muffled whispers of the pilgrims who visit there and when I felt their emotions, I realized that it was more of a shrine than it is a venue for tourists, just another stop in a crowded day of "doing" Manhattan. For millions of immigrants, it was the gateway not only to the New World, but to a veritable new world of identity, an identity as an American citizen. People come to Ellis Island every day, especially white Americans, hoping to find a connection to history by uncovering or reexperiencing their ancestors' past. I have to confess that I envy my friends who can go there and discover their family's journey from Europe to the United States in the early decades of the twentieth century. All they have to do is know the name of one of their ancestors who immigrated to this country, type that name into a computer, and, like magic, they can access a record of the day on which that person arrived here! They can even pay a hundred dollars to get a copy of that record and to have their ancestor's name inscribed outside, on a wall of immigrants, a veritable Who's Who of European immigration to this country in the early quarter of the last century. I wish it were so for all Americans.

Unfortunately, there is no Ellis Island for those of us who are descendants of survivors of the African slave trade. Our ancestors were brought to this country against their will. When they arrived, they were stripped of their history, their family ties, and their cultural and linguistic identities. And we, their descendants, have been unable to learn much about our African heritage until very, very recently.

This fact has shaped me as a person and as a scholar. I have been obsessed with my family tree since I was a boy. I regretted the fact that the slave past had robbed me of so much knowledge of my

ancestors—of the privilege of knowing even their names. I remember when my grandfather Edward Gates died in 1960. I was
ten years old. Following his burial, my father showed me my grandfather's scrapbooks. And there, buried in those yellowing pages of
newsprint, was an obituary—the obituary, to my astonishment, of
the oldest known Gates ancestor, our matriarch, an ex-slave named
Jane Gates. "An estimable colored woman," the obituary said, also
mentioning that she had been a midwife. I wanted to know how I
got here from there, from the mysterious and shadowy preserve of
slavery in the depths of the black past. I became obsessed with my
family tree and peppered my father with questions about the names
and dates of my ancestors, which, ever so dutifully, I wrote down in
a notebook.

I knew I had white ancestors. My father, his six brothers, and
their sister were clearly part white. "Light and bright and damned
near white," my dad used to joke. I wanted to learn the names of
both my black and my white ancestors. As I got older, I especially
wanted to learn the name of our white patriarch, the white man
who impregnated my great-great-grandmother Jane Gates. I
wanted to see my white ancestors' coat of arms! I remember as a
child, we used to look at ads in the back of magazines encouraging
the reader to send in his or her name and receive by return mail, for
twenty dollars or so, one of those colorful European coats of arms,
the sort one would see hanging on the wall of a castle in England. I
thought about ordering one for the Gates family. I knew it wouldn't
have anything to do with me, necessarily, but who knew for sure?
Perhaps I was related to these white Gates people, someone such as
the Revolutionary War general Horatio Gates. Slavery had robbed
"the means of knowing," as the great black abolitionist Frederick
Douglass once put it, from most black people who were descended
from a white ancestor.

I even allowed myself to dream about learning the name of the very tribe we had come from in Africa. (I have to confess to certain delusions of grandeur: I was hoping that we were descended from African chiefs, not just any old Africans! And who wouldn't want to be? If not an African chief, then most certainly an Indian chief!) When Alex Haley's *Roots* came along in 1976, I had one serious case of roots envy. I became an historian, in part, I think, out of this desire to know myself more fully, which, of course, over time became a desire to understand others as well, to learn about the past of my people, my black kinsmen, and, through their stories, to learn about the past of the African American people, and, ultimately, the past of my nation—at least my own genealogical tributary of this nation. Finding my own roots has been my lifelong quest ever since my grandfather's funeral. And the passion to learn the names of my ancestors was never very far beneath the surface of my motivation to become a scholar. When I was an undergraduate student at Yale, I determined that one day I would know—at least I would work hard at knowing—who, and what, "my people" had been.

After decades of being frustrated by my inability to trace my family back beyond slavery—back to one maternal ancestor in the Gates family line—I decided to do something about it. So I invited eight prominent African Americans to allow their family histories to be researched for a documentary film series for PBS. We traced their families, combing over every anecdote we heard and every little scrap of paper we could find—and when the paper trail would end, inevitably, in the abyss of slavery, we would then try to find their African roots through the science of DNA. It was a risky experiment—no one had tried this before—but it turned out to be a remarkably rewarding experience. I called upon scholarly colleagues from various disciplines—professional genealogists, state-of-the-art DNA researchers, top-notch historians—and invited them to help me. They joined this quest willingly, even eagerly.

I learned one thing very quickly: sifting through the detritus of

African American genealogical history is a complex task, one that can challenge the expertise of even the most patient and well-trained expert. So many of the most interesting and compelling family stories about our ancestors passed down over Thanksgiving or Christmas dinners, or at family reunions, turn out to be more wishful thinking than fact, sometimes containing a kernel of truth, but many times not! In the process, working with these experts, I learned a great deal—about African American history, about American history, but primarily about myself, deepening my understanding of the African and African American past, certainly, but even more, deepening my understanding of myself, of who I am as a person. I believe that this was true for the eight other subjects in my television series *African American Lives* (which aired in February 2006), including Oprah Winfrey, Quincy Jones, Whoopi Goldberg, Chris Tucker, Bishop T.D. Jakes, Dr. Ben Carson, Dr. Mae Jemison, and Dr. Sara Lawrence-Lightfoot.

But a PBS documentary goes by in a flash. It's a few hours long and then—*bam*—it's over. And there was so much more that I learned and wanted to talk about that I couldn't fit into the series. So many people, black and white, have come up to me on the street or in airports since the series aired, asking important questions. The most common question is this: "How can I do this myself; how can I trace my own roots?" To help them answer this question, I decided to produce another PBS documentary, titled *Oprah's Roots,* and, more important, to write this book to show how to construct a family tree—anyone's family tree—by looking at the family history of one of the world's most famous black Americans: Oprah Winfrey. Even I wanted to learn how "Oprah Gail Winfrey," a descendant of illiterate slaves in Mississippi, dirt-poor scratchers of the soil, became the inimitable Oprah, a cultural icon wherever human beings can watch TV or film. I wanted to work my way back through time, starting with the Oprah millions of us watch on TV every day, and ending somewhere, I hoped, in Africa, centuries earlier.

Why Oprah? Well, I had two main reasons. First of all, Oprah fascinates me, as she apparently does just about everyone else on the planet. I admire her tremendously for what she's accomplished and who she is. She's *sui generis*. There's never been anybody in history like her, and I wanted to know how this compelling person became one of the most popular and fascinating individuals in the world. I wanted to know where she got her uncanny sense of the zeitgeist. When I was a teenager, we used to tell a joke about James Brown—we'd say that James Brown knew what the average black man was thinking just by waking up in the morning. And then he would set whatever that was to music. He could feel the pulse of the black community without even trying, seemingly unconsciously. James Brown was Black Everyman, if not Black Everywoman.

I think Oprah, somehow, is as close to Everywoman as any human being has ever been, for white people and black people and just about every other shade of people, and for males as well as females. I wanted to know where that came from—what her family tree might tell us, if anything, about the source of this extraordinarily rare capacity for empathy and communication. Of course, there's no way to know for sure. There never is. There are millions of biographies of famous people, and none explains its subject fully. Yet each can teach us something, bringing us, perhaps, just a little closer to an explanation that makes sense of how a hero becomes a hero. And that's what I set out to do here: get a little closer to an understanding of what makes Oprah tick by looking at her ancestors.

Although it's vulgar to say that we are our ancestors, or that who we are individually is the result, primarily, of the traits and characteristics and personalities of our ancestors, there is something that is, at the same time, so obviously true about that statement that most of us simply take this for granted. "Who are his people?" My father, at ninety-three, still asks that question when I introduce him to a new friend. It's almost embarrassing to have to say it, but we are an extension of our pasts, our own and that of our family. We are not trapped by our pasts, thank goodness. Our life choices aren't delimited or predetermined by the choices that our ancestors made. But we are, in part, inevitably the product of our past, our individual pasts and our collective past. That's one of the reasons so many of us furiously swab our cheeks for our DNA: to learn what our "pasts" reveal about our present, indeed, about "us." We all look to antecedents in an attempt to understand what makes each of us individuals, what makes us unique, certainly, but what also ties us to a common past, even if that past is only as broad as the branch of a family tree. Paradoxically, none of us wants to be imprisoned by the limitations of our family's history; rather, we seem to want to use knowledge of that history as a springboard to new possibilities, as both a comfort zone and an enabling mechanism, a set of facts necessary for a certain psychic comfort, but not sufficient for foreclosing our individual life possibilities.

My second reason for wanting to look at Oprah's family history was more complicated. At bottom, I think, I had a suspicion that it would be a most fascinating story—and more than that, that it would provide a cogent and compelling means through which to interest a wide array of people in the larger issues of the American past and the importance of genealogy, especially black genealogy, within that past. As I've said, these subjects are dear to me. And Oprah herself is fascinated with them. She told me once that she thinks it's crucial for African Americans to understand their family history—and she speaks eloquently about the importance of understanding our grand history, our collective history, in terms of that family history. "Knowing your family history," she says, "is knowing your worth—your whole worth. And I don't mean your monetary value. It's about everything that everybody gave up for you. It allows you to know what your mama went through, your grandmama went through, your great-grandmama went through, your grandfathers. It lets you know that you have been paid for— that there are lots of people who come before you who would have liked to have had what you have. I think about this all the time— you know, my ancestors could not have imagined the life that I now lead but the work that they did prepared the way."

I couldn't have said it better myself.

I met Oprah Winfrey through my friend Quincy Jones. When I got the idea of creating the PBS series *African American Lives,* it was Quincy whom I phoned first. Quincy had written the musical score for the television mini-series *Roots,* and Alex Haley became one of his best friends. Since the airing of *Roots,* Quincy had become a student of genealogy, engaging the services of Johni Cerny, who came to specialize (largely because of Quincy's gift of family trees to many of his friends) in African American genealogy. The idea was to do *Roots* for the twenty-first century, using twenty-first-century techniques such as the Internet and DNA analysis to trace the ancestry of a small group of African Americans, all the way from the tomb of slavery in America, well, back to our nameless past in Africa, to the heart of "the Continent," as we call it, the Motherland of all black Americans, which now, most scientists believe—thanks to DNA analysis—is the Motherland of us all. The question is not if we came from Africa; the salient question is how recently? All human beings are "Africans," if only we search far enough into the past.

Quincy agreed right away to be one of my subjects. On the phone, I asked if he would help me to secure the cooperation of his best friend, Oprah Winfrey. He agreed to assist me but told me that I had to ask her myself. So I sent her a letter describing what I was trying to accomplish in the series and how I planned to go about it.

A week later—it was a Sunday afternoon—my phone rang. My Caller ID informed me that Quincy Jones was on the line.

"Hey, Q!" I exclaimed. "What's happening?"

"Dr. Gates?" a female voice asked.

"Yes," I said, realizing, My God, it's Oprah Winfrey.

"I would be honored to be in your TV series!"

Man, that was, as Carter G. Woodson might have said, one happy day for the Negro! With Quincy and Oprah on board, I believed I had a chance to make a new kind of documentary series about not just the African American Experience but also about the history of the human community, how eight extraordinary people came to be who they are in the twenty-first century—first, out of the deepest recesses of the evolutionary past, and more recently, out of the darkness that has beclouded the contributions of black people to American history.

I spoke with Oprah for a few minutes, promising her that I could trace her family tree back through slavery by drawing on the skills of a whole team of talented people—genealogists and historians. She was intrigued. Then I asked her: "What if we could even travel through time across the Atlantic and find where your African ancestors came from, what tribe your mother's line descended from?" It's such a powerful question for all African Americans. What Alex Haley had attempted to do through the oral tradition, I told her, scientists are now claiming that they can do through DNA analysis. This journey would have been unimaginable just a few years ago, but thanks to miraculous breakthroughs in genealogy and genetics, this remarkable process has begun, a process that we might think of as "reversing the Middle Passage." After all this time, there exists the very real possibility of learning the names, at long last, of our African ancestors' ethnic groups, or tribes. How amazing would that be?!

Oprah was incredibly excited. And I was incredibly nervous. I knew I was promising a lot—and there were huge challenges in front of me. Now, I had to deliver.

There are so many obstacles for African Americans who want to trace their family trees. Slavery is, of course, the biggest. Slavery was, among many other things, a systematic effort to rob blacks of all family ties and the most basic sense of self-knowledge. With very few exceptions—and there were some, oddly enough—each slave had one name only, a first name. No matter what a slave called him- or herself, and no matter what their family and friends knew them by, the American legal system did not generally acknowledge those names. Good luck building a family tree for somebody who has only one name.

But, of course, slave owners didn't want their slaves building family trees. They didn't want them to marry or maintain deep, abiding relations with their mothers and fathers, their grandparents, or their siblings or friends. They wanted them to feel no bonds of kinship. Why? Because a family unit is a bond—and an extended family is a larger bond—and out of such bonds, loyalty and resistance are built. And the last thing in the world slave owners wanted was resistance. Accordingly, with very few exceptions, the slaves had only one name that the legal system acknowledged, if it acknowledged their existence as human beings at all. That's what happens when you are property, or when the larger society defines you that way. *Uncle Tom's Cabin* was originally titled *The Man Who Was a Thing*. And turning a human being into a piece of property, a thing—the attempt, at least—begins with stripping away a person's name, which is their language or mirror onto the self. For an individual, taking away one's name is the equivalent of taking away an entire group's language, its window on tradition, on heritage, on its collective past.

Oprah is very aware of these issues. For someone who is not a trained historian, she is incredibly well versed in African American history. And like most African Americans, she didn't really know who her ancestors were because such knowledge is so difficult to come by. As she said when we started our first interview, looking at old records that drew us back into slavery: "I know I come from this. I don't know their names and backgrounds, but I know I come from this."

As I explained to Oprah, if you want to build a family tree, you must necessarily start in the present and move back through time, discovering your ancestors, their lives and the times in which they lived by writing down their names as your elders tell you who they were. To do this, you need to do oral history. You need to talk to the people in your family who raised you, with whom you spent years living, whom you saw virtually every day as a child. It can be a very emotional experience. I told Oprah it would be something like writing her autobiography—and that she'd end up thinking about things she hadn't thought about since she was a child. She's told segments of her life story many times before, of course, but this time would be different. And this is true for anybody who wants to do their own genealogical research. You need to be willing to look at your life afresh. You need to start in the present, with yourself, and write down everything you know. And then you need to work back in time, from your parents to their grandparents and beyond. It's a fascinating process, one that will reveal much more than just names and dates. But it has to be done methodically.

"You start with what you know," says my expert genealogist

friend Jane Ailes, repeatedly, like a mantra. "And if all you know is your parents, that's where you start, and you go one generation at a time. Don't leap way back and look for a family story that says, 'Oh, we were owned by so-and-so.' Instead, listen to that, throw it aside, and then just work one generation at a time and learn everything you can about each generation. Don't get in too big of a hurry to get back to the Civil War." It's excellent advice. You have to be painstakingly exact as you grow your own family tree. You have to follow every generation back, looking at every aunt and uncle and cousin you can, trying to learn with whom they associated, where they lived, what they did to earn a living. Don't move on to the next generation until you feel comfortable with what you've uncovered about the one you're working on. Just take your time. There are so many little things that can trip you up. People get married and change their names, or they move, or they take a nickname or tell a lie to the census taker. Stories can change over generations. Even the spelling of a family name can change. So you have to do every-thing systematically and take a lot of notes, and just try to keep everything sorted out.

Tony Burroughs, another remarkable genealogist, also gave me some fine advice on this. "As a story gets handed down from gener-ation to generation," he said, "there's a tendency for things to get changed, left out, edited and moved around. Unfortunately for novices, they believe every word of oral history is fact. And that's not necessarily the case. I recommend you take everything with a grain of salt. Ask yourself: 'Does it sound reasonable, does it sound not reasonable, is this something I can verify?' Do not take the po-sition that you believe it unless you find something else. Take the position that you take it with a grain of salt, see what you can ver-ify, and be leery of everything else." As an historian, I can say a loud "Amen!" to that.

So I strongly advise you to bring along your skepticism when you do your research. But bring your sensitivity, too. There are so many little things that might seem random to an ordinary person which may actually turn out to be extremely useful to a genealogist. Somebody might say, "I remember being at so-and-so's funeral, and I don't think anybody ever put up a gravestone." Is that useful? It sounds so vague. And yet, you can go to that cemetery and maybe there's no tombstone, but there might be some church records or some funeral home records. There might be somebody else in the family who remembers the funeral or even has an old diary that says, yes, I was there at so-and-so's funeral, or a family Bible that records the date of an ancestor's death. You just never know. But pretty soon, you start putting together all kinds of little things and it starts to fall into place. Your family's past, and your relation to it, will slowly emerge, bit by bit, from these tiny little details, details seemingly unimportant on their own.

I cannot stress enough the importance of this kind of painstaking research, which can be remarkably fecund, yielding all sorts of new leads for a genealogist to pursue. Of course, the stories that families tell themselves about their past aren't always reliable—or even always true. So many family tales reflect wishful thinking or family myth-making, "remembering" things the way we would have wanted them to be rather than the way they actually happened. I think of it as "voodoo" genealogy: George Washington was Abraham Lincoln's daddy, as Mr. Charlie Carroll of Piedmont, West Virginia, used to say! Zora Neale Hurston once joked that she was the only Negro she knew who wasn't descended from a Native American chief! And many of us today still cling to this sort of myth of origins, especially when it comes to our putative Indian antecedents, including relatives in my own family. In fact, DNA evidence reveals that most African Americans have very little, if any, Native American ancestry, as common sense would dictate, if we only paused to think about it for a minute.

But as genealogist Tony Burroughs says, we need to collect oral history because we "need the stories in their heads. They don't exist in any library, archives, or courthouse, so you interview them." It can be a very exhausting process. But it can also be incredibly worthwhile.

Despite its limitations and dangers, you just can't do enough oral history when you are starting to research your family tree. Often these family stories—the stories that our elders tell us at family reunions or over ritual family dinners such as Thanksgiving, Christmas, or Kwanzaa—are, in fact, historically accurate, to some degree, containing a kernel of truth that can be built upon by diligent research. And there's no other way to get at this information, because the sad reality of our community's past is that many of the most important and poignant stories about our people have not made it into the pages of African American history. So you should be ready to gather as carefully and as painstakingly as possible as many anecdotes and memories as your family members are willing to share. You'll throw out a lot, eventually; nevertheless, the narrative that you'll ultimately assemble will be constructed, necessarily, on these oral tales. Some wheat will emerge from amid a lot of chaff.

We live in a world so very different from the world inhabited by our parents and grandparents; to understand them, we need to listen as carefully as we can to their stories, and then to test them against the available historical record. Memories form the building blocks of family history. They are the stories that survive in our kitchens and in our living rooms, stories that "tell it like it is" about "the way it was," the way things used to be—or at least stories that try to. Some are humorous. Some are preposterous: One of my own newly discovered relatives, for example, on the Redman side of my family, contacted me recently and claimed that our common ancestor was a slave in the Shenandoah Valley (before any European settlers had even arrived in that region of Virginia!), and that this ancestor not only escaped his captors but found refuge among the Iroquois people in what is now Hardy County, West Virginia, where he took an Iroquois wife with whom he had twelve children. Not only that, but some of these twelve children, half Iroquois, became scouts for General Braddock and General Washington during the French and Indian War, because their father—my ancestor—had been murdered by the Algonquin people, so they were seeking revenge. The problems with this marvelous tale of heroism and sacrifice are that no settlers of any kind lived in this region when my cousin claims some of this occurred and that no Iroquois or Algonquin people lived at this time in what is now eastern West Virginia! It is a good story, though; it just happens not to be true.

Other family stories are so painful, even embarrassing, that they have been repeated only in whispers, if at all. But all of these family tales make up the essence of African American history, and none—in the early stages of the research process, at least—should be excluded or ignored. So write down everything your relatives tell you, even tales about your Choctaw great-grandfather, or, in my own case, my half-Iroquois patriot scouts.

A word of caution, though: Running right alongside a rich tradition of storytelling, there is also, in the black community, a very understandable history of self-censorship. And you're probably going to face this when you do your oral histories. I've interviewed many people over the years who've spoken about a kind of shame or reticence in the black community. For example, many survivors of Jim Crow don't want to talk about it. Further back in time, many survivors of slavery didn't want to talk about that, either, for the most understandable reasons. It was a nightmare to be a slave, even on the best of days. A slave's degree of vulnerability is difficult for us to fathom today. Then, too, as quiet as it is kept, there is a certain degree of stigma attended to being a slave, even among black people. I have met well-educated, middle-class black people who have actually claimed, out loud at cocktail parties, let's say, that they have no slave ancestors! And that's a very interesting kind of self-censorship you don't hear much about.

Black self-censorship started with slavery and extended well into the twentieth century. Talking about slavery was incredibly difficult, especially when a person somehow thought that his or her enslavement was, somehow, his or her own fault. Think of this as the guilt of the victim. In addition, many people have thought that talking about slavery or segregation reinforced the stereotypes of black people as helpless and hopeless, that our ancestors' enslavement constituted an almost complete sort of subjugation of the self, even if these stereotypes are not true. And people just did not want to perpetuate these sorts of stereotypes. So lots of African Americans have found it especially painful to reflect honestly and openly upon the past. Ours was, in part, a history of subjugation too horrendous to grasp. Survivors of slavery and then Jim Crow were akin, in some ways, to Holocaust survivors. It's no accident that it took forty years for someone to make a film such as *Shoah* (1985). It is no accident that the first history of slavery written by a black historian, from the point of view of the slaves—John W. Blassingame, Sr.'s *The Slave Community*—was not published until 1972, five years before *Roots* aired. Nothing good came out of slavery, it was argued, so nothing good could possibly come from remembering slavery. It wasn't until the 1930s that oral testimonies of ex-slaves were systematically collected on a large scale, and even so, it would take decades before these narratives would find their way into history books as valid historical evidence. Many historians dismissed their value out of hand, claiming that the slaves were "biased"! After all, what could a slave possibly be able to testify about their own enslavement?

But if you want to build a black family tree, you need to get beyond all this. You need to shine a light into the past, reticence be damned. You must be sensitive, you must be aware of how painful some of our past can be, but you must push through to the fundaments of recollection. Accordingly, you must begin your genealogical research with a very thorough oral history—by setting down your own memories and then by asking questions of your family members who are still alive and can remember back generations before you. And I would strongly advise that after you do your own oral history, you next turn to the oldest people in your family. It's important to talk with them because you want to capture their memories while there's still time—and those memories will guide your questions to the younger generations. As a matter of fact, older family members are most probably the source of these stories, which younger generations repeat with lapses, embellishments, and variations. It's also very important to interview each of your subjects multiple times, to get as close as you can to their real life story as well as their memories of relatives and ancestors. Memories shift in the telling, so capture a relative's story from as many angles as time will allow.

What kind of questions should you ask? It's a good idea to start by collecting a list of basic data. Ask about people's parents, siblings, and distant relatives. Ask about jobs and property, marriages and birthdays. Get as much concrete information as you can. You'll be comparing it to the historical record later—to census data, death certificates, and the like. So you'll need good hard information. As my genealogist friend Johni Cerny says: "There's no truth without proof," which means that you can't make assumptions based on a few facts or a few good stories. Genealogy is a discipline, like a science, and you have to back up everything you hear with hard evidence that you'll later find in the public documents.

So be prepared to check every scrap of oral data. And I mean that you really have to roll up your sleeves and conduct some serious historical detective work. To match the oral history against the public documents takes a lot of care and effort. If you're going to get serious about your genealogy, you need to dig a lot deeper than the Internet for ten minutes—or even what your local library has lying around in its archives. As the genealogist Tony Burroughs says: "You need to go through the family archives, the basements, the attics, the trunks, the shoe boxes, the dresser drawers; you want to look and find anything and everything that has the mention of a relative or ancestor's name on it—like the family Bible, photograph albums, obituaries cut out from the newspaper, funeral programs, certificates, diplomas, all kinds of things that are buried around the house that will give you bits and pieces and clues that you won't find anywhere else. From there you want to go to the cemetery where your ancestors are buried, understanding that you want to locate the grave markers that are there but also understanding that not everybody could afford a grave marker. In other words, there are records within the cemetery for people who didn't have grave markers. So you want to see if there's a sexton office. If not, you want to find out who owns the records for the cemetery as well as go to the funeral home, get records from the funeral home which are separate from the cemetery, and then you want to get death certificates, birth certificates, marriage records, and that helps piece you back step by step by step."

Sound like a dizzying roller-coaster ride from hell? Well, it's not. It's history. More important, it is your family's history, and, ultimately, your own. Finding the ancestors—any ancestors—on one's family tree can be extraordinarily exhilarating, and is incredibly worthwhile, a small but significant contribution to our larger knowledge of the American past, as well, of course, as of the past that you, as a person, embody and represent. The more effort you expend, the more results your labors will yield. As Jane Ailes says: "There are some people who do genealogy just to fit a bunch of names together. I think that's dull and boring. If you're going to find out about the ancestors, let's find out who they were as people— not just when they were born or who their parents were or where they lived. Let's find out something about them—their occupations, the land that they owned, the family they married into, the relations they had with their siblings and cousins, who their neighbors were, who they associated with."

As you'll see in the stories about Oprah Winfrey's roots, Jane Ailes was right—all those little connections can bring your ancestors back to life, or as close as anything possibly can. Genealogy is a way to honor the dead by keeping their memory alive.

PART TWO

Oprah

Oprah Winfrey's birthplace, Kosciusko, Mississippi, in a photograph from the late 1940s. Oprah spent the first six years of her life here with her maternal grandparents, Earlist and Hattie Mae Lee. *From the personal collection of Thomas Craft*

*A*fter a couple of sleepless nights, I began my real work on this book by flying to Chicago to interview my subject: Oprah Gail Winfrey, born January 29, 1954, in Kosciusko, Mississippi. I asked her to tell me her life's story, hoping it would lead me to clues about her ancestors. I got a lot more than I bargained for.

As we talked, I saw clearly that Oprah's family experience had shaped her profoundly. Moreover, I saw that the stories of her family's past offered an intriguing way to look into the larger American past. I began to have all kinds of thoughts—some familiar, some totally new—about the African American experience, as glimpsed through the prism of Oprah's heritage. My mind was constantly racing about, conjuring images of all that has been hidden from us, all that we've presumed to be excluded from the annals of our shared history as a people. Indeed, the history of Oprah's family, like that of almost all black people, has been determined largely by the racial context in which they found themselves—in times of slavery, Civil War, Reconstruction, segregation, black codes and Jim Crow, the Civil Rights Movement.

And many blacks were trapped by these supraforces—pulled down by racism like the force of gravity; pulled down by injustice, to paraphrase Dr. King, like the waters of a mighty stream. So many of our ancestors were given so very few choices over their lives. Rather, their choices were delimited by the larger economic and political contexts in which they found themselves, within the even more pervasive sphere of antiblack racism. Nonetheless, they persevered. And some succeeded wildly, like the woman in front of me, and, as I would later discover, some of her direct ancestors. There are always exceptions in history. And as I spoke with Oprah, my mind was almost exploding with the rich tension between the exceptions and the norm, between the major thrust of African

American history and the precious few who were able to take a different path, who were able to "get over," as we say. My thoughts were going in a hundred different directions. I guess that's what an historian does when he or she is engaged. It's part of the process of grappling with history. I will try to capture some of it for you.

Oprah's life today is a far cry from the rural poverty of her southern youth. When she was a girl growing up in Mississippi, her grandmother used to say to her: "What you want to do is grow up and get yourself some good white folks." Oprah enjoys this irony and was excited to take a journey into her past—excited, in part, because she has done so much to honor and embrace African American history. Indeed, black history almost breathes from the walls of her home, graced as they are with all sorts of black artworks, historical documents, and memorabilia. I asked her why this history was so important to her, and the answer came easily. "It's important to me because it is who I am," she said. "I realized that there was a life beyond the front porch in Mississippi when I started reading about Sojourner Truth and Harriet Tubman and Mary McLeod Bethune. To me, all that was a connection, a connection to me. It was a bridge to the here and now." I smiled in agreement. "You can't be an evolved person," she said, "without understanding where you have evolved from. And I have always, even when I could not explain it, felt a deep, deep connection to those who have come before me. When I was a little girl growing up, as soon as I was able to read, I started reading about African Americans. I remember the first time I read *I Know Why the Caged Bird Sings*. That was the first time I thought, There is a story about me! And it said to me that my life and what happened in my life mattered."

When I asked her about her parents, she immediately became quite animated. They are an absolutely integral part of who she is today. Her father, Vernon Winfrey, was born in 1933 and was twenty-one years old when Oprah was born. Her mother, Vernita Lee, was nineteen when Oprah was born. Vernita was born in Kosciusko, Attala County, Mississippi, just as Oprah was, while Vernon was born in nearby Carroll County, and they both came from families that had been in the area since the days of slavery. They never married. And like many African Americans of their day, they both fled the rural South looking for better economic opportunities in northern cities. In fact, Oprah's parents were part of the largest population shift in American history, what we call the Great Migration.

At the dawn of the twentieth century, African Americans were predominantly poor, southern, and agrarian. Seventy-five years later, we had migrated to every region in the nation and were occupying virtually every profession. Sparked by an industrial boom during World War I, blacks were lured to northern factory jobs. They were also escaping the racism, segregation, and the racial terror, violence, and—perhaps as important—fear of arbitrary violence that primarily defined black-white relations in the South from the Reconstruction period between 1866 and 1876 to the end of the Civil Rights Era, with Martin Luther King's death a century later in 1968.

The Great Migration changed the face of the country from rural to urban, and changed the complexion of entire sections of these cities from white to black. When southern blacks flooded cities, they changed the identity of African American culture as well as the landscape of America as a whole. Sharecroppers became factory workers. Black people abandoned farm life, nature, and the horizon and crowded into all-black high-rises; the "dark ghetto," as the great sociologist Kenneth Clarke put it, was born. The black middle class was born, too, because the Great Migration was a narrative of ascent, of progress. And that was certainly the case for

Oprah's father, Vernon Winfrey. He went into the army, got an honorable discharge, and moved north from rural Mississippi—a hotbed of segregation and racial violence—to Nashville, Tennessee, taking along the work ethic that he had learned on his father's farm. It helped him to purchase the barbershop that he still owns today.

"I was looking for better opportunities," Vernon recalls. "So I came to Nashville with my mind set on taking up a trade. I didn't finish high school until I was twenty-five years old. And I missed a couple of better paying jobs after I was in Nashville because I didn't read as fast as I should have. So I had bad jobs, low-paying jobs. And so I emphasized to Oprah the need for getting something that no one can take from you. She complained sometimes about other children dressing better than she did. She mentioned that a young lady that lived right nearby dressed better than she dressed. And I said to her, 'You get something here'"—pointing to his head—"and you can dress like you want to in days to come. And everything worked out. She can dress pretty good now if she wants to."

Vernon smiles as he recalls his daughter's successful career, in obvious and very understandable parental pride. But his smile smoothes over a deeper, more troubling story. By the late 1950s, Vernon was finally reaping the benefits of his hard work. He owned his own barbershop in Nashville—which he still owns, and at which he works every day—and his own house. He had moved from the rural South into the stable and comfortable black lower-middle class, and he had married. But his good fortune didn't extend to his daughter.

Oprah had a terribly difficult childhood. Her mother, Vernita, moved to Milwaukee in 1954, the year in which Oprah was born. Her father was gone soon after. But Oprah stayed behind and was raised by her maternal grandparents, Hattie Mae Presley and Earlist

Oprah's father, Vernon Winfrey, with a customer at his barbershop in Nashville,
Tennessee, in the late 1950s. Vernon was one of countless African Americans
who fled the deep South in the years after World War II, looking to escape the
institutionalized poverty and racial violence of the Jim Crow era.
From the personal collection of Vernon Winfrey

Lee, until she was six years old. Oprah has curiously poignant memories of the isolating effect that the Great Migration had on her family. "I remember being a little girl and going to visit my father in Nashville," she says. When she returned to the South, the adjustment was a painful one: "And my grandmother was always saying, 'Where you been?' Because whenever you went up North and you came back people would say, 'You tryin' to talk like you from up North.' And so my grandmother was hurting my feelings. And I said, 'I've been to the city, Grandma. I've been to the city.' And she said, 'You look like some city.' I understand now that she was sad because she felt like I was going to become attached to the city—and that she was going to lose me."

Oprah had little understanding of why her family had been torn apart. She was told that her mother had moved to Milwaukee to have "a better life" there. She was told that her mother was living with a cousin—which may have been true for a while yet did not give the full picture. She grew up confused about basic aspects of her family. But she has vivid, formative memories of those years she spent with Hattie Mae. And even then, Oprah always believed that she would achieve more than her grandmother could have achieved.

"When I was growing up," she said, "I remember standing on the back porch and looking through the screen door and my grandmother was boiling clothes in a big, black pot. It must have been winter because I could see the vapor from her breath and she had the clothespins in an apron on her sash and I was churning butter. I was supposed to be churnin' anyway, so I was churnin' and every time she'd turn around I'd churn and then when she was not looking I would stop churning and she said, 'Oprah Gail, I want you to pay attention to me now. I want you to watch me because one day you're gonna have to learn how to do this for yourself.' And I watched and looked like I was paying attention but I distinctly recall

Oprah Winfrey with her maternal grandmother, Hattie Mae Lee (*far right*).
Hattie Mae taught Oprah to read and was a seminal influence on her.
From the personal collection of Katharine Carr Esters

a feeling that no—I'm not—that this will not be my life. She worked for a white family and used to always say to me, 'What you want to do is grow up and get yourself some good white folks. You want to get good white folks like me.' Because her white folks let her bring clothes home and many of the things that we had came from her good white folks. And I think her idea of good white folks was just that they give you things and you get to bring food home. But I also think it meant for her that you at least got to keep a piece of your dignity—a piece—and that's the best you could do. And so she'd say, 'I want you to grow up and get some good white folks.' And, you know, I regret that she didn't live to see that I did get some good white folks workin' for me, yeah. She couldn't imagine this life."

Although Oprah was only a child, she was experiencing first-hand the rural poverty that drove so many African Americans northward and the sinister forces of racism that permeated every aspect of life in the Jim Crow South. The historian James Horton has given me incredible descriptions of this time period, conjuring a world of such injustice that it is often difficult for students today to accept that this was real. "Not only was it dangerous to live in the South if you were black," says Horton, "but it was socially uncomfortable. You were forced to drink from certain water fountains, sit in certain parts of the bus. And some of these Jim Crow laws were just unbelievable. Do you realize that there was a law in Atlanta that a white witness and a black witness could not swear on the same Bible? In North Carolina there was a law that said in a factory, workers, black and white, could not look from the same window. I mean some of these laws were just incredible." Before Oprah was old enough to endure the full humiliation of Jim Crow segregation, her mother insisted that she join her in the North. And so the six-year-old girl moved to Milwaukee. The difference between life in

Oprah Winfrey's mother, Vernita Lee, in a photograph taken sometime in the early 1960s, after Vernita had moved from Kosciusko, Mississippi, to Milwaukee, Wisconsin.
From the personal collection of Oprah Winfrey, © *Harpo, Inc.*

Mississippi and life in Milwaukee was enormous—and the experience was deeply traumatic for her.

Before the move, Oprah says, "I had no relationship or memory of my mother whatsoever. I'd only been raised by my grandmother. I knew I had a mother, but all those years my primary relationship was with my grandmother and all of a sudden just one day I'm packed up and put in a car and told, 'You're gonna go live with your mother now.' It was horrible. But something inside me clicked. I knew that I was going to have to take care of myself. I felt and have always felt really independent and now that I didn't have my grandmother anymore, I knew I was gonna have to take care of myself."

In Milwaukee, Oprah's mother was collecting welfare, working as a maid to earn a bit of extra money, and starting a new family.

"My mother had another child," remembers Oprah. "And she was living in the home of a woman named Miss Miller—and Miss Miller was a colored lady but a very light-skinned colored lady who did not like colored people." Oprah began to cry at the memory of those days.

"I remember being there," she says, "and I instantly knew that Miss Miller did not like me because of the color of my skin. I was too dark and I was a nappy-headed colored child, and Miss Miller would say it. And my half-sister Pat was five years younger than me and she was light skinned and my mother was staying there because Miss Miller loved my half-sister. And I was put out on the porch to sleep. There was a little vestibule, like a porch area where you came in and left your shoes before you went into the house and so that's where I slept. I wasn't even allowed in the house to sleep. It makes me sad to think about it. And it was because I was brown skinned and it didn't compute for me because my mother was brown skinned, too. But I realized she was okay because she had Pat."

I found this story very moving—deeply illustrative of the horrible ways that African Americans have internalized racism, the ways we've visited pain on one another. The story is an unfortunate but vital part of our collective history, a story that, sadly, is shared by thousands and thousands of people. We've been color struck. I've participated in it myself. I remember, as a kid, being proud that my father was a mulatto—his whole side of the Gates family was light. Many of them even looked white; some could—and did— "pass," and they had "good hair," straight hair. And I thought that was wonderful. I was also proud, as the barber would have said, that my brother and I had a "mixed grade" of hair—hair that wasn't really kinky, and certainly not straight, but that had a basic wave to it. These values—light skin, straight hair—were all very good things for a colored person to have when I was growing up. You didn't want to look like Nat King Cole, even with his beautiful process. You didn't want to be dark complexioned. I remember my great-aunt Pansy Gates Thompson. She looked like a white woman; in fact, she was so white that she looked like a ghost with blue eyes, my father would jokingly claim. And she, with other black women who were educated and who had married professional men, and who, by and large, were light complexioned, was part of a bridge club called the New Jersey Matrons. They all had almost no black ancestors, as far as they were concerned. They thought their ancestors were all white people and Indians—with maybe one remote black person thrown in somewhere. I even heard one claim that there had been no slaves in her family, as if her African ancestors migrated here in the seventeenth century through Ellis Island, willingly, three hundred years before there was an Ellis Island! This sort of delusional family history was self-willed mythology, a sign of a certain form of self-hatred. But it was painfully commonplace among many black people, especially among the black bourgeoisie.

Oprah remembers that she understood this situation the minute she walked into the house where her mother was living. When children's reactions and instincts haven't been ruined by the adults raising them, they can be quite keen. Oprah's certainly were. Nevertheless, she was powerless to change things, to act on her perceptions or to alter her mother's landlady's harsh treatment of her mother's darker, kinky-headed child.

Between the ages of six and fourteen, Oprah moved back and forth between Milwaukee and Nashville, alternating between the homes of her mother and father, growing ever more isolated. "I was sent back and forth," she told me. "That whole part of my life was

An elementary-school photograph of Oprah Winfrey, taken after she went to live with her mother in Milwaukee, Wisconsin, where she would attend an integrated school and flourish as a student. However, Oprah would also be sexually abused between the ages of nine and fourteen. *From the personal collection of Oprah Winfrey,* © *Harpo, Inc.*

about going back and forth from one parent to the next. So I never developed deep roots or connections to either parent because I never knew at what time I was going to be pulled from one to the other. It was just arbitrary. They'd decide this summer you're going to go here and then next summer you're gonna be here and now you're living here, now you're living there, and I remember grades because I loved school so much. So I lived with my mother for first grade, lived with my father for third grade and fourth grade, skipping the second grade."

The summer after fourth grade was a turning point in Oprah's life.

"I was nine years old and got sent back to Milwaukee for the summer and ended up staying there because my mother had said that she was going to marry her boyfriend and we were going to be a family. But the summer of my ninth year, things changed immensely for me, because I was raped and then kept that secret for a long time while living with my mother. I was raped by a nineteen-year-old cousin—who my mother was also living with. And then I was molested by the boyfriend of my mother's cousin. He was a constant sexual molester of mine. And I just felt like this is what happens to you. I felt like I was marked, somehow. I thought it was my fault. And I had no therapy—none. I was actually doing a show in Baltimore in the early eighties, a talk show, and another black woman was on who talked of being raped by her uncle. And I thought I've never heard of that before; I thought I was the only person that had ever happened to, and it was very lonely and I knew in my spirit that it would not have been safe for me to tell. I felt instinctively that if I told I would be blamed, you know, because those were the days when people said, 'Well, you were fast anyway, you know?' Or else,

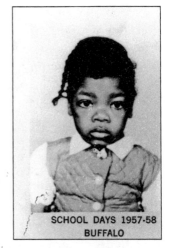

**SCHOOL DAYS 1957-58
BUFFALO**

Oprah Winfrey, age three, when she was living with her maternal grandparents in Kosciusko, Mississippi. *From the personal collection of Oprah Winfrey,* © *Harpo, Inc.*

like Pa says of Celie in Alice Walker's novel *The Color Purple,* 'She always did lie.'

"And so I was sexually molested repeatedly from the time I was ten to the time I was fourteen in that house. My abuser practically told everybody. He'd say, 'I'm in love with Oprah. I'm gonna marry her, she's smarter than all of you.' He would say it and we'd go off to places together. Everybody knew it. And they just chose to look the other way. They were in denial. And then there was this sick thing going on—my cousin who lived with us was also a battered woman. And I used to bargain with her boyfriend that he could have sex with me if he wouldn't beat her. I felt protective of her and I'd say, 'God, okay, I'll go with you if you promise not to beat Alice.' And that's how it was."

Alone, with no one to trust or confide in, Oprah's adolescence became a living hell. She wouldn't fully understand the profound trauma of these events for many years. Indeed, there was a time in the black community when it was commonly argued that sexual abuse occurred only in white families, just like suicide. "I was about forty when I stopped thinking it was my fault," she said. "I got all my therapy on the *Oprah Winfrey Show.*"

School was Oprah's only respite—a place where she could feel safe and in control. Oprah says that she always thought she would become a teacher. Her grandmother Hattie Mae had taught her to read at an early age. "And having grown up with my grandmother reading," she recalls, "I went to my kindergarten class, and the first day of kindergarten, I was so bored. I thought, I'm gonna lose my mind with these kids sitting there with their ABC blocks. So I wrote my kindergarten teacher a letter. I sat down and I wrote: 'Dear Miss New.' And I wrote down all the words that I knew. I said, 'I know words.' I knew Mississippi, hippopotamus, Nicodemus, Shadrak, Meeshak, Abendigo. I wrote down all the big words I knew. And so she said, 'Who did this? Who did this, girl?' And I got marched off to the principal's office and I got put in the first grade the next day. And then they skipped me to third because I was such a good reader."

This was an integrated school. Oprah never went to a segregated school. But Miss New was a black teacher. And the fact that her first teacher in kindergarten was a black teacher deeply impressed her.

"If she had been white," asked Oprah, "would I have had the courage to write that letter? I don't know. I remember going home and saying, 'I have a colored teacher.' And she was colored like me. She was brown skinned. So I felt like I could connect to her and that she would understand me. And so I got myself out of that kindergarten class."

Stepping back from the story of Miss New, Oprah began to talk about the central role of education in her life. "The one element," she said, "the prevailing element in my life that has allowed me to not be embittered or feel discriminated against is that I had education. And so I never felt less than a white kid. White people never made me feel less. Black people made me feel less. I felt less in that house with Miss Miller. I felt less because I was too dark and my hair was too kinky. But when I was in school, I could walk in any classroom and I was always the smartest kid in the class.

"I had great teachers," she said, "who made me love learning. And they didn't discriminate against me. They just rewarded me because I was smart. I was always the kid with my hand up—always. And I felt empowered by what I knew and what I was curious to learn. And, you know, if you're a teacher, the kid in the class who's excited about learning is the kid who you're going to go to. So people thought I was the teacher's pet, but I was just excited about learning new things all the time. Teachers need motivated students because it stimulates them. Now I know that, but at the time I didn't know that. And this is what I found out: Teachers tell other teachers. That's what they're doing in that teachers' lounge. And so by the time you get to the fifth grade the fifth-grade teacher has already heard about you. I was a star!"

Hearing Oprah talk about her early schooling was deeply moving, reminding me of how I felt so very comfortable as a student in the classroom, even in elementary school. I was particularly struck by the contrast between the reinforcing climate that she discovered in her school and the alienation that she experienced within her home, especially hearing the horrific stories of her sexual abuse.

The very idea of education transformed her—school had clearly given her an enormous amount of self-gratification and self-assurance. At the same time, school could not protect her from the trauma of daily life in her mother's house.

After recalling so warmly the sense of self generated by her performance in school, she soon returned to the subject of the consequences of her sexual abuse. By the time she was fourteen, she said, she was living on the streets of Milwaukee. "I became a sexually promiscuous teenager," she recalls. "I ran away from home. I was going to be put into a detention center and ended up being sent to my father instead. I was out of control."

Oprah's father provided a lifeline. His sense of the need to impose authority, the order and financial security of his Nashville home, and the role model provided by his new wife all combined to give Oprah discipline and stability—her last chance to save herself. All of this would lead to a profound transformation.

As her father, Vernon, recalls: "I just had my rules, and you had to go by my rules, and she appreciates that today. She's told me that if I had not been a strict disciplinarian, she would be somewhere maybe in public housing with a bunch of babies. She's thanked me several times for it."

But Vernon offered more than stability—he offered a renewed focus on education, reinforcing an earlier passion for learning that abuse had served to obscure.

"On the Winfrey side of my family," Oprah recalls, "education was such an important part of what my grandfather believed in, even though he wasn't well educated. This is one of the things that he passed on to my father. I mean, my father graduated from high school and didn't go to college, but in my household education was everything. I remember coming home once and I had a C and my father says: 'Cs are not allowed in this house, you know, you are not going to live in this house.' And we were sitting in the kitchen and he opened the door and said, you know, 'You can stay out there with those people if you're gonna bring a C,' he said, 'because you are not a C student. You are not a C student! If you were a C student, I would let you get Cs, but you're not a C student so you can't bring 'em in this house."

Oprah's life changed completely when she moved back to Nashville. Her father didn't know her deep, dark secrets of her time with her mother, but he knew she was troubled and he tried to restore order.

"My father knew I was out of control," she said. "He made an announcement in the house when I came back: 'The rules are gonna change. If you make the decision to run away, then you will stay away. You're going to have a curfew. The curfew will be obeyed. You will bring in the grades that you are capable of bringing in.' You know? He just really sat me down and we had that conversation."

Oprah laughed at the irony of this memory—at the painful remembrance of what she survived. Her father could not imagine the true depths of her problems or their origin. "He said to me that there would be no association with boys. He didn't know there had already been association. Because I was pregnant when I came to my father and my father didn't know it. So he sat down and said to me that he would rather see a daughter of his dead floating down the Cumberland River than to bring shame on the Winfrey name. And I knew I was pregnant. I thought about killing myself. All I thought about was dying and how could I kill myself."

The stress caused Oprah to go into premature labor. Her legs started to swell and her father sent her to see a doctor—accompanied by her stepmother, Zelma Winfrey.

"My father said, 'I don't know. Her legs are swelling.' So my stepmother takes me to the pediatrician and I'm at the pediatrician's office and the pediatrician is looking at me and I'm probably five, six months pregnant, and he says, 'Either this is the biggest tumor I've ever seen in my whole life or you're pregnant. Are you pregnant?' And my stepmother was there in the room. And so I said, 'No.' And so he asked my stepmother to leave the room and then I broke down and cried and, oh, my God, it was—it was bad."

Oprah then had to go back home and tell her father. She doesn't recall what he did or said, only that he was devastated by the news and that she was overwhelmed with shame, falling further into a deep depression, consumed by thoughts of suicide. The story is harrowing—and its ending was tragic. Oprah went into full labor shortly after seeing the doctor, and delivered a baby that would die a few months later. With that, her father took full control.

"My father," she recalls, "came in and said to me, 'This is your second chance.' He said, 'We were prepared, Zelma and I, to take this baby and let you continue your schooling, but God has chosen to take this baby and so I think God is giving you a second chance and, if I were you, I would use it.' "

I asked Oprah how she could possibly survive this ordeal at the age of fourteen. I am not sure that I could have. She replied, quietly, that she didn't know. The emotion that she remembers clearest was shame—the profound sense of shame she felt over the pregnancy and her efforts to hide it, which she describes in a way that vividly evokes the world of her youth. "Now I think girls get pregnant," she says, "and, you know, it's not the same deal. It's not the shaming, most embarrassing, horrible thing on a family as it was even when I was in high school. I mean, I went back to school and not a soul knew. Nobody. Otherwise I would not have had this life that I've had. If anybody had known, I would not have been vice president of the student council. I would not have been oratorical champion, I would have not been voted most popular, I would not have had all of the access and opportunity that was offered to me. I mean, when I was a sophomore in high school, I was picked by the State of Tennessee out of all the teenagers in the state to attend the White House Conference on Youth. That would not have happened to me. None of it. Because I remember in my high school senior year, the first girl that got pregnant that everybody knew about, there was this big brouhaha whether she would even be allowed to graduate and be able to walk with the rest of the graduating class. And the de-

Oprah Winfrey's 1971 yearbook photograph, taken while she was a student at East Nashville High School. By this point, Oprah's life had begun to blossom under the stabilizing influence of her father. *From the personal collection of Oprah Winfrey,* © *Harpo, Inc.*

cision was no, she could not walk with the rest of the graduating class. So my entire life would have been different. Entirely different."

Though her survival may be a mystery, even to her, Oprah has often credited her father for being the source of her transcendent success. And, clearly, he played a profoundly significant role in reshaping, indeed, resurrecting, her life. I asked Oprah what she thought of her father after all these years. Did she think of him as a terrible authoritarian or was he a loving, kind, sympathetic person? Her response was profoundly perceptive, and honest.

"He was both," she said. "My father is not sympathetic or nurturing. The best way to describe him is as an honorable man. He is filled with great discipline. I've never seen him not go to work. I mean to this day, he's still working in a barbershop. He's probably behind the chair right now. But he really was the guiding force in my life, my father—and my stepmother, to whom I really have not paid enough homage: If it were not for my stepmother, the discipline and the kind of ethic that I bring to my work would not exist. It would not have been possible because she helped my father to nurture that. See, she was not a schoolteacher; my father loved schoolteachers, so he would say over and over, 'Zelma has three years of college and she almost finished the fourth year.' And so for him, education is everything. Everything." Oprah's father's reverence for education, embodied in his wife's example, inspired her to achieve, to excel in the classroom.

As it turns out, thanks to her father's discipline and her stepmother's encouragement, Oprah won a scholarship to study speech, drama, and English at Tennessee State University. At the age of nineteen, she began coanchoring the news at Nashville's CBS affiliate, WVTF. And by 1977, she had moved to Baltimore's ABC affiliate, WJZ, before taking a new job in Chicago, seven years later, which would catapult her to the unimaginable heights she has since obtained.

Learning all of this, hearing Oprah tell me the story of her young life, enabled me to begin to see how she had been shaped—positively and negatively—by her family. And I wanted to find out more about these various family members, about who had raised them, where and how, under what circumstances. Remember, this was just our first interview, the first necessary step in beginning to

Oprah Winfrey in the late 1970s, with her father, Vernon, stepmother, Zelma, and cousins, Judy, Carla, and Burnice Winfrey, Jr., at a wedding in Nashville, Tennessee. *From the personal collection of Vernon Winfrey*

Seventeen-year-old Oprah Winfrey being crowned "Miss Fire Prevention" by the Nashville Fire Department in 1971. Despite the hardships and sexual abuse she suffered as a young girl, Oprah underwent a remarkable transformation in her teenage years, thanks to her father's discipline and her stepmother's encouragement.
Nashville Fire Department

trace the contours of anyone's family tree. In Oprah's case, I wanted to learn how many strands of her story could be found in the lives of her ancestors to whom she had introduced me in these anecdotes, ancestors whose names I had written down: Vernon and Vernita Winfrey, her parents; her educated stepmother, Zelma; her maternal grandparents, Hattie Mae Presley and Earlist Lee; and Vernon's parents, Elmore Winfrey and Beatrice Woods. From this interview alone, I knew her immediate ancestors' names, where and when they were born, when and where Oprah was born and raised, and some of their occupations. While this might not appear to be a wealth of information, my researchers and I would soon be able to see not only the trunk of Oprah Gail Winfrey's family tree but also several of its low-hanging branches. And this would be enough, already, to take us back to the early years of the twentieth century. With this foundation, we would then begin the much more difficult process of climbing from the twentieth century back into the late nineteenth century of Oprah's family's past.

Thus, perhaps unwittingly, by this point in our interview, Oprah had given me a wealth of data from which we would be able to discover even more generations of ancestors both in Oprah's father's line and in her mother's line. With these data, I was becoming optimistic that we might even be able to penetrate what I think of as the sound barrier to black genealogy, the slave past that ended only with the cessation of the Civil War. But we'd have to see if it would be possible to connect Oprah's ancestors from the early years of the twentieth century back to the decade of Reconstruction and beyond. This can be a tricky process, but it can be done.

PART THREE

Into the Past

*T*racing your family back two generations is usually not too difficult, even for an African American. The twentieth century has left us with a wealth of records to help us explore the lives of our grandparents: newspaper articles and obituaries—buried in the rich soil of microfilmed local black newspapers and magazines, published as early as 1827, thriving through the nineteenth century, and surviving well into the twentieth century—land deeds, marriage licenses, census records, as well as birth and death certificates, along with records found in family Bibles and in the records of churches and funeral homes. And these can be matched—again, carefully and meticulously—against our own memories and the memories of our living relatives. Indeed, building Oprah's family tree was made much easier because Oprah knew her grandparents so well, and because of her ability to give me a lot of useful information about them. She also was fortunate that her father is still living, as are a number of cousins and relatives who proved to be a fertile source of anecdotes and memorabilia. In the end, everything she told me about her grandparents, I was able to confirm or adjust based on the historical record and on the conversations I later had with her relatives.

Her maternal grandparents were Earlist Lee, born in 1887 in Hinds County, Mississippi, and Hattie Mae Presley, born around 1900. Oprah lived with them for the first six years of her life. They had a tremendous impact on shaping her childhood, perhaps even more than was usual for someone of Oprah's generation.

As Oprah had told me, her grandmother Hattie Mae taught her to read. "She was barely literate," says Oprah, "but she understood the Bible. And we had a set of Bible stories. And so she would tell me the stories and then I learned to read by memorizing what I thought the words were. And aside from really creating this desire to read, my spiritual roots come from that. I remember that my grandmother and I, every night, we would say our prayers together. And my grandmother would say, 'For as long as you're able, get down on your knees, the Lord likes you better when you're kneeling.' And that has stayed with me. Even last night, I was so tired, I got into bed—then I got out of the bed to get down on my knees."

Oprah was able to describe her grandparents' daily life in vivid, eloquent detail. "I slept with my grandmother in a big poster bed in the living room," she said. "We had a hearth and the living room had the bed in it. There was just one big room with the hearth, the bed. People would come to visit and there'd be the chairs in front of the bed. We called it the front room. And behind the front room was the kitchen. There was no running water. And to the side was another room where my grandfather slept.

"My job in the morning was to go to the well and bring water. And to take the one cow out to pasture. And my job was then to do whatever it is my grandmother wanted me to do—get the eggs from the chicken without breaking the eggs." Because she was the youngest member of the family, Oprah was given many small undesirable tasks to do. "When it was hog-killing time, I was the one picking up all the intestines and I would flick things off here and there. I had all the worst jobs."

She remembers her grandmother making lye soap and homemade shoes, and sewing their clothes: "It was a really big deal to get store-bought clothes or patent leather shoes," she marvels. Hers was a daily routine of grinding work. "During the course of the day," she said, "you had to do everything. If you wanted water in which to bathe—I only bathed on Saturdays—and if you wanted water to drink or to bathe, you'd have to go get it. If you wanted food to eat, you'd have to grow the vegetables. I remember going down the rows, dropping the seeds in. I remember when it would come time to pick the vegetables, I'd be out there picking the greens and the turnips, the collard greens. It was a rural life. There was no indoor plumbing, no bathrooms, of course. And I had a great big fear of the outhouse. I always thought I was going to fall in! It was my job to empty the slop jar in the morning. We had the slop jar under the bed. It was my job to keep the irons clean—because we had those irons for ironing clothes and so when you used starch, they'd have to be washed off and scraped. It was my job to do that. I was a busy little girl."

Hearing her talk, it is astounding how far Oprah has come— yet she is right; the rural poverty she describes was typical, indeed pervasive, among black people in the South. Oprah grew up surrounded by sharecroppers, people bound to the soil by a system that was intended to replace slavery with its mirror image, a system of peonage to which most blacks were chained economically, as surely as they had literally been chained in slavery. The vast majority of former slaves became sharecroppers almost as soon as slavery ended, and very few were able to break out of this system and own their own land. Oprah's ancestors, as we shall see, proved to be the rarest of exceptions.

It's important to understand how seemingly hopeless the system of sharecropping was. It flowed directly out of the nightmare of slavery. Viewed from one angle, the system itself might seem to have been fairly innocuous—and its deeply tragic effect on the black community might be overlooked. For most black people, sharecropping was an economic disaster, the effects of which Oprah's grandparents felt in the 1940s and '50s—in some ways, those economic effects are still felt today. It is part of the great betrayal of the freed slaves. Remember, blacks emerged from slavery with no real means of self-support. They were nominally free, but they were living in an overwhelmingly agricultural society and they didn't own any land. Many of them had the skills to earn a living, to grow crops and sell them, but without a farm of one's own, those skills have limited market potential.

So the sharecropping system evolved, ostensibly to address this problem. It allowed poor, landless farmers—almost invariably blacks—to work the fields of large and small landowners in exchange for a stake in the crops (hence the name sharecropper). Now, this system might have benefited all concerned *if* it had been administered fairly. In theory, it provided a means of profit for both the former slave and the former slave master. But the problem was that all the power was in the hands of the former slave holder. The landowner made almost all decisions about what crops were planted, how the harvest was priced and marketed, and how much the sharecroppers were rewarded for their labor. This led to myriad inequities. Most sharecroppers had to rent their land at exorbitant rates, the plantation owners set wages however they liked, and they also controlled all the things that farmers depended on—the supply stores, banks, and tool shops as well as the police forces, judges, militias, and local governments. They held all the cards.

Accordingly, while sharecropping may have seemed to be a good deal for African Americans in theory, in practice it was just a new form of slavery, backed up by racism and violence that could be as terrifying as that of the pre–Civil War days, with lynchings, beatings, and Jim Crow laws replacing the old slave system. Whereas under slavery, black people had no assets; under sharecropping, they plunged into an abyss of indebtedness. As the historian Angela Hornsby describes it: "What we see with sharecropping is African Americans spiraling into a debt which was very difficult to get out of, because, in actuality, they were not in receipt of the benefits from the system. So every season, we see African Americans needing to basically go to community stores, to take out cash advances, to make purchases on credit, which normally had exorbitant interest rates of more than thirty percent. And because of that, African Americans subsisted in a cycle of debt which was very difficult to get out from under. And this was enforced by whites, through economic means, and through violence."

The sharecropping system held southern blacks in poverty for almost a century after the Civil War. Education was a way out of this poverty—for many, it was the only way out. And it was for this reason that blacks fought for the right to educate their children as if their lives depended on it—which, in some ways, it did—and why many whites systematically attempted to foreclose those opportunities, or severely limit them. It is not an accident that the primal battle of the Civil Rights Movement—*Brown* versus *The Board of Education of Topeka, Kansas* (1954)—was fought in the Supreme Court over the integration of public schools.

As we have seen, Oprah's father, Vernon, understood this and he and his wife, Zelma, encouraged the education of their children as strongly as they could. Unfortunately, Hattie Mae, Oprah's maternal grandmother, had a different imaginative horizon, a horizon delimited in scope by the confines of the sharecropping system, Jim Crow segregation, and its various complex legacies. No doubt because of this set of experiences, she could not imagine encouraging her granddaughter to dream of getting an education so that she could become a doctor or some other kind of professional (as so many African Americans dreamed for their children). Instead, Hattie Mae wanted Oprah to grow up and "work for good white folks." And, given the severe limits of her own options, this was a noble enough aspiration to have.

But on the other side of Oprah's family, her paternal grandparents narrated to her—and embodied—a remarkably different story.

Oprah's paternal grandfather, Elmore Winfrey, was born in

1901 in Poplar Creek, Mississippi, to Sanford Winfrey and Ella Staples. He had eight siblings. In 1925, when he was twenty-four, Elmore married Mattie Mae Carson. They had their first child in October. We know this from records stored in Holmes County and Carroll County, Mississippi. What happened to that marriage and to that child is unclear. There are no further records of them. But on June 10, 1925, Elmore married Beatrice Woods in Carroll County. Beatrice was twenty-two. Were the two marriages overlapping? We don't know. We do know that Elmore's marriage to Beatrice endured. They had nine children together, including Oprah's father, Vernon Winfrey.

Oprah knew Elmore and Beatrice. Though she saw them rarely after she left Mississippi, she heard plenty of stories about them from her father, and these stories accord with the records we've been able to find—land deeds, marriage licenses, and obituaries.

Her grandfather Elmore was a farmer, and, according to Oprah, a great talker, too, a riveting storyteller. "I remember my grandfather's stories," she said. "We know where I got that. He was a talker. That's what I remember best."

We were able to find out much more about Elmore. Jane Ailes spent five days in Mississippi and immersed herself in the records and in the courthouses, interviewing all kinds of people, going to the library and even to the cemetery, seeing the Winfreys' graves—visiting all these places to get the "feel" of Oprah's family history. This research—as well as historical research into the period—served to enhance Oprah's memories, an ideal step in the reconstruction of any family history. Fortunately, a full, robust picture emerged.

Elmore grew up and lived much of his adult life in the Jim Crow South—where economic opportunities for African Americans were exceedingly scarce. As we have seen, the vast majority of

Oprah Winfrey's paternal grandparents, Elmore and Beatrice Winfrey, in the 1980s. *From the personal collection of Vernon Winfrey*

black farmers were sharecroppers, and their lives were brutally harsh. Most sharecroppers were illiterate. And most whites wanted it that way. If black farmers couldn't read or count, then they couldn't manage their own transactions. That made them vulnerable, and they could be taken advantage of. Indeed, if you look at contracts between blacks and whites written in the Jim Crow years, blacks were often paid less than their fair share. However, there were exceptions, including by all accounts Elmore and Beatrice Winfrey. Elmore could read and write and understand math. He was reportedly a good businessman who successfully managed his own farm.

In the 1920s and '30s, southern farmers, both black and white, were struggling economically. It was hard times all around. Drought and the cotton-destroying boll weevil pushed many farm owners into bankruptcy and drove their workers off the land. There are many gaps in Elmore's story, but the public records of June 1925 show Elmore living one county over from his original residence in Poplar Creek. Had he moved because of the terrible economic conditions of that time? Did he spend the Depression years as a sharecropper, exchanging his labor for a small percentage of the crop? Or was he a tenant farmer, renting the land on which he worked? We don't know. What we do know is that he managed to make money. We found a land deed revealing that in 1942 Elmore spent $3,425 on a 104-acre piece of land, ten miles southwest of Poplar Creek. This is truly remarkable for a black person who lived at his time, either in the North or in the South, but especially in the South. As we shall see, Elmore's purchase of land was very much in the Winfrey tradition.

Oprah was not at all surprised by this news. "I've heard great stories," she said, "about my grandfather being the businessman that he was." She's also heard all about the vicious racism that surrounded the lives of her grandparents and their neighbors—and how education offered the only way out of this morass. "My father," she said, "often tells this story about my grandfather not wanting his wife and daughters to have to go and work for the white man or work in the white man's kitchen because he understood, many times, that, you know, Mr. White Man would be abusing those women, and that there would be nothing that he could do about it. And so what he always wanted to do was to be able to be the provider in such a way for his family that he would never have to put the women in the family in that position. And he understood that education was the open door to freedom for all of them. So thanks to him, all my father's siblings were well educated, and every time I went to their house, that's all anybody ever talked about. 'So-and-so was in school, so-and-so's finishing school and graduating, so-and-so's going to college.' It was where I got that belief system. It came from that part of the family."

Oprah appreciates the struggle Elmore must have endured to preserve his status, as should we all. We tend to forget, from the vantage point of the twenty-first century, that it was a tremendous accomplishment for a black man or woman to be successful at the height of racial segregation and not be trampled, robbed, or killed. The Klan was very active throughout the South, and very dangerous. One of their principal targets was, inevitably, blacks who owned land, or even aspired to do so. You see, the promise of America, as the great Yale historian John Morton Blum once wrote, was land. White people migrated to this country from the very beginning so that they could acquire land, which they could not acquire, by and large, in Europe. Only males—white males, initially—who owned land could even vote in this country! There are well-known cases of black middle-class settlements being destroyed by white vigilantes throughout the South, from Rosewood, North Carolina, to Omaha, Nebraska. And owning land was the conduit to middle-class status, because it implied economic stability and promised mobility, the mobility of subsequent generations.

Racism, in America at least, was ultimately about economics. It wasn't primarily about skin color. Skin color, what we commonly call race, was the metaphor for deeper economic relationships. Slavery and subsequent race relations in America were always, at bottom, fundamentally about who was going to get the biggest share of the economic pie, and which source of cheap labor could be exploited most expeditiously to ensure that certain people enjoyed that larger share of the pie. This is why sharecroppers replaced slaves in the great chain of economic exploitation. For a black man or woman to be able to purchase land, and to hold on to it, was one of the truly great accomplishments in the history of the African American people, especially in the South. In Oprah's case, not only did her direct Winfrey ancestors own land, but they retain it to this day. And in so doing, they commanded respect from their white neighbors.

We talked to Oprah's father, Vernon, about this very subject. All through Oprah's life, he had told her stories about his father being able to walk through town with his head up. But we can only wonder what it cost him, in terms of his humanity, in terms of his "manhood," to be able to do so in the Jim Crow South.

Vernon told us a remarkable story. He said that whenever Elmore encountered white people, he would tip his hat and say, "Yes, sir" and "No, sir." Vernon believed that his father felt compelled to do this, of course, and that he was a man who valued manners as well. But this embarrassed the young Vernon. Vernon was something of a Young Turk—bolder than his father and ultimately unwilling to accept the racism of Jim Crow Mississippi. In his eyes, his father, however great a businessman he may have been, was still tipping his hat to the white man. And that made his father an Uncle Tom. Young Vernon couldn't accept this.

But years later, Vernon would be shocked to learn that his father, Elmore, had decided in 1965 to house two civil rights workers in a back bedroom of his home. This was the year that the Mississippi Freedom Summer became the "summer of blood." Vernon couldn't believe what his father had done, how much of his economic stability and security he was willing to risk to further this political cause, which he had been seemingly oblivious to for decades.

According to Vernon, the sheriff came to Elmore—a white sheriff, of course—and said to him, "You're one of the most respected negras in this area. Now other black people think that you're sending the message that it's okay to support the Civil Rights Movement." And Elmore replied, "Well, if you want to know what message I'm sending, go to that Civil Rights March on Sunday because I'll be sitting in the front row, sending my message—it's time for a change!"

Oprah had never heard this story before I told it to her. And it surprised her, the same way it astonished her father when he first heard it. It was like her grandfather, certainly a mild-mannered man, conservative in his habits, if not exactly filling Vernon's description of him as an Uncle Tom, had become a fiery black militant, seemingly overnight.

"Well, that is like Malcolm X," Oprah said, astounded. "I mean, for him to be able to say that to the sheriff's face—and live. That was a lynchable offense. To actually house the civil rights workers and then to have the guts to say that to a white man's face? They must have had a lot of respect for him."

We could not confirm Vernon's account of his father's conversation with the sheriff, but we were able to track down the two civil rights workers whom Elmore housed—Luther Mallet, who in 1965 was a fifteen-year-old African American living in his native Kosciusko, and Matthew Rinaldi, who was a nineteen-year-old white college student from Long Island. Both testify to the role Elmore played in the movement in Mississippi.

"Those of us in the Civil Rights Movement could not have existed without the tremendous support that we received from the local black community," said Rinaldi. "People fed us, people housed us, people protected us, and people gave us empty houses to use as freedom houses. And one of the families that housed me and fed me up to that point was the Winfrey family, Elmore and Beatrice Winfrey. Mr. Elmore Winfrey was a strong supporter of the Civil Rights Movement."

Rinaldi then happily recalled his first meeting with Elmore and

Beatrice. "They were totally welcoming," he said. "They made me feel right at home. They ushered me into a large bedroom—told me that was where I could stay and I bedded down for the night in this double bed. And frankly it was not until the next morning when I saw Mr. and Mrs. Winfrey sleeping out on the couch that I realized they'd actually given me their bedroom to stay in. I couldn't do that. And we had a conversation about it. They were extremely gracious. But I said, 'I'd be happy to sleep on the couch.' I simply could not take their bedroom. And so from that point forward I slept on the couch and Mr. and Mrs. Winfrey had their bedroom back. But, you know, they took a big risk putting me up because this is not a big town and people certainly knew where I was when I was at their house. They put themselves in a position where retribution was possible at any time. But they were willing to take that risk. They were very generous, very courageous people."

Mallet was equally vivid in describing the racism of Kosciusko at the time, giving detailed context to Elmore's decision to aid the Civil Rights Movement. "Growing up here," Mallet said, "I attended all black schools, and when you would go to town and stuff like that, we always had to tilt our head down when we was on the sidewalk and move to the side. There was no black restaurants. When you wanted something to eat, you would go to the back door. You had to go to the back door or you'd go to the front and call someone to come and bring you something. There was blacks in the kitchen cooking but there was no blacks inside the restaurants. And there were no economic opportunities. None. We picked cotton. We plowed, bailed hay—and people all left and went up north, Chicago, Detroit, Milwaukee. You know? Just to leave. There was no opportunity here. If you was here, you was suppressed here."

We asked about the white backlash against the civil rights workers in the area. Neshoba County, where the Klan killed three civil rights workers in 1964—Andrew Goodman, Michael Schwerner, and James Earl Chaney—is only forty miles southeast of Kosciusko, and racial violence was widespread across this area. Elmore risked death by defying the sheriff with the language that he used. Heroism and courage come in small actions as well as large. It is difficult for us, today—even for African Americans—to comprehend how stifling, how oppressive, how restricted were black life choices in the American South throughout most of the twentieth century. And how dangerous it was to assert one's self, even—or especially—in the form of lending support in any way whatsoever to the Civil Rights Movement.

Mallet remembers drive-by shootings and the need to carry a rifle for safety. Rinaldi recalls intense and constant threats: "The dominant force in the white community," said Rinaldi, "was hardcore segregationists—Ku Klux Klan—ready to use violence against us. The first visit here, we were attacked by two car loads of armed white men who shot up the freedom house and actually wounded two of the students. And Mr. Winfrey and Mrs. Winfrey were targets of the Ku Klux Klan, and the word here was that at one point a cross was burned on their lawn by the Ku Klux Klan. I have no direct knowledge that that actually happened. But a lot of what goes on or went on in those days in Mississippi has to do with rumor and innuendo, and if the word was simply put out that a cross was going to be burned on their lawn, that in and of itself constituted a threat. And Elmore and Beatrice Winfrey were also greatly at risk. They knew this story. They knew that they were at risk and they did not let that stop them. And that's very important."

Mallet also remembered Elmore's bravery. "Mr. Winfrey lived right across the street," he said. "And often he would talk to us. With his striped overalls and his straw hat and a smile on his face, he was a very church-going but also a real strong man when it comes to civil rights. Being that his house was on the main street, he still stood up. And that was vulnerable for someone to do anything at any time. But it never bothered him."

Rinaldi closed our interview by adding another piece of information about Elmore, describing how after a freedom house in nearby McCool, Mississippi, had been burned down by local whites, Elmore used his carpentry skills to help rebuild it, making the dangerous trip between Kosciusko and McCool even as armed Klansman were traveling the same roads. "Elmore was very calm," recalled Rinaldi. "And when you're in a dangerous situation as we were, had we been working with somebody who was also nervous and showed that nervousness, it probably would have intensified our own fears. But it was the opposite. Mr. Winfrey seemed unflappable. He had made his decision that he was gonna do this work. He knew he was gonna be driving back and forth from Kosciusko to McCool on a daily basis, which posed a danger to him. But you never had the feeling that he was scared. You never had the feeling that he thought he was at risk. And his calmness was contagious."

Rinaldi also provided us with an array of archival material from the time, including pictures of Elmore helping to rebuild the freedom house. Oprah had never seen these images—and they moved her to tears. She herself has few memories of the Civil Rights Movement. She was, of course, too young, having been born in 1954. She retains early impressions, though, and—like so many people of her generation—vivid memories of the 1963 March on Washington and Martin Luther King's astonishing speech. She remembers watching the news that night and thinking that she wanted to be Dr. King. "I thought," she said, "I want to do that, I want to lead a march. I wasn't thinking like I wanted to go to that march, I was thinking: Oh! I want to *do* that one day!" Little did she know that her own grandfather had exhibited an enormous amount

Oprah Winfrey's grandfather, Elmore Winfrey, using his carpentry skills to help rebuild a Freedom House in McCool, Mississippi, in 1966. The house had been burned down by local whites. *From the personal collection of Matthew Rinaldi*

of courage by standing firm, in his own way, in his very own household.

After talking with Oprah about her grandparents—the Lees and the Winfreys—my ability to learn about her family from her own memories, including recollections she'd heard from her family as a child, had reached its limit. She never knew her great-grandparents. Her recollections could take me no further back. I had to pursue other leads, other avenues into her family's past.

When memory runs out, a genealogist must rely entirely on the historical record. But as our researchers started looking for documents to take us past Oprah's grandparents, they discovered something that every historian dreads: Oprah's ancestors lived in counties in Mississippi that suffered huge losses of records in the 1800s. The courthouse in Choctaw County burned three times, the last time in 1881. The courthouse in Attala County burned in 1857. Fortunately, the courthouse in Montgomery County did not burn. Nevertheless, when you are trying to research a person from Poplar Creek, which is in Montgomery County, this problem arises: Montgomery County was formed from Choctaw County in 1871, and the Choctaw recordings prior to 1881 were lost in courthouse fires. And you can't replace those records.

So what could we do? Well, fortunately, the Kosciusko-Attala Historical Society in Kosciusko, Mississippi, had preserved some of the records. We also consulted old regional newspapers, such as *The Kosciusko Messenger,* which provided a wealth of anecdotal information. Even more important, there are state records and federal records that can give us information the county records can't. And this is an important reminder to any would-be genealogist: It's essential to know what kind of information is contained in each different type of record and where those records are stored. For example, in Mississippi, birth and death certificates are stored at the state level, not at the county level. So we were eventually able to locate a lot of those at the state capital.

The U.S. federal census also contains a wealth of information and every census taken prior to 1930 is now available to the public. The easiest place to access census data is on a website called Ancestry.com, but it is subscriber based. Fortunately, often your local library will own a set of the census records for your immediate area, or possibly your entire state. The federal government has them, too, of course. If you visit the National Archives in Washington, D.C., or one of their regional archives throughout the United States, you can gain easy access to all of the census data you need to trace your ancestors. In addition, many libraries and the Family History Centers in the Mormon churches provide their patrons with access to Ancestry.com and Heritage Quest databases. Often, the Heritage Quest databases can be accessed from home, free of charge, by using your library card as a password. (You can ask for details at your local library.) Other free and subscription databases are available online, and your local librarian can direct you to these.

Our researcher Johni Cerny took me to the Family History Library of the Church of Latter Day Saints in Salt Lake City, Utah, where they have collected an incredible number of genealogical records from all across the country. In Salt Lake City there are more records of human beings than in any other place on earth—three billion deceased human beings are recorded at the Family History Library. Three billion. Some scientists estimate that only 100 billion human beings have walked the face of the earth, and the Mormons have records of about 3 percent of them. That is mind-boggling! No matter one's ethnicity, race, or religion; no matter one's ancestor's point of origin, this library is an invaluable resource for building a family tree. It's packed from 7:30 in the morning till 9:00 at night.

The facility contains 2.4 million rolls of microfilm and more than 300,000 books, filled with not only census records, but also estate records, land deeds, church records, baptismal records, city directories, and phone books. They even have microfilm copies of thousands upon thousands of self-published books containing inventories of cemetery tombstones. Who knew that there are people out there willing to go write down every inscription on every tombstone in their local cemetery? (Some ambitious souls have even inventoried entire counties worth of cemeteries.)

What's more, there are no significant access restrictions to the library's collections. Anybody can walk into the place and find out about births, deaths, marriages—anything that contains statistical information about an ancestor's life. It astonished me the first time I visited there, early on a Saturday morning, and it astonishes me just as much each time I return to undertake research. The intense concentration of the researchers, often just normal people eager to find information about their own ancestors, and the bursts of excitement shouted out when someone is fortunate enough to discover a new fact about someone in their family, endear this sanctuary of family history to me.

In Oprah's case, we were extremely fortunate here. We were able to search land deeds and marriage records that gave us a wealth of information about the Winfreys, as well as a few school records and court records from Montgomery County. We also perused draft registration records, some of those tombstone books, and a wide variety of estate records. We reached many dead ends but we learned a great deal, too.

I was also lucky in that Oprah gave us permission to talk to her cousin Katharine Carr Esters, who's kind of Oprah's unofficial family historian and for decades has done a wonderful job gathering historical material from her relatives regarding their ancestors. Katharine's work was invaluable and helped make up for all those lost records in Mississippi.

What we obtained, in the end, was a further wealth of information about several fascinating individuals—information that reinforced some repeating motifs that help us to understand how Oprah Gail Winfrey came to be Oprah. We have seen how important the motif of education was to Oprah's childhood. Judging from its role in her ancestors' lives, education is just in Oprah's "genes," as the saying goes. (I wrote earlier about "voodoo" genealogy; well, *voodoo genetics* is another term that comes to mind whenever I hear people say that a trait or propensity or a characteristic or a habit of mind is in one's genes—of course, these sorts of traits can be "passed down," but through one's environment, through the ethos that one imbibes from one's family and even from extended relatives, through day-to-day contact. These traits are in the air one breathes along with one's family, in the proverbial "mother's milk." And education is one such characteristic even for the distant ancestors of Oprah Winfrey.)

Looking for Hattie Mae's mother—Oprah's great-grandmother on her maternal line—we found Amanda Winters, born around 1874 in Kosciusko, Mississippi. Most of what we were able to learn about Amanda we first gathered by talking with Oprah's cousin Katharine, another example of how crucial family stories can be. Katharine was enormously informative, providing us with a wealth of information about Oprah's maternal line.

Amanda was the daughter of Pearce and Henrietta Winters, both former slaves in Mississippi. She attended a Freedmen's School; for their time, she and her siblings were quite accomplished individuals. Her brother Jesse Winters attended Wilberforce University and her sister, Matilda, was a math teacher. Amanda herself taught public school English to black children in the 1890s and

1900s. The terms of the school were only four months long, because the children had to be available to return to the fields to pick cotton when harvesting season came. (Education was a virtue and a value; but cotton was valuable, too: it fed everyone, it paid the rent.) With teaching came status in the community—and a family. Amanda married Nelson Alexander Presley in 1893. (We have found no relationship between Nelson Presley and Elvis Presley's ancestors.) They had eight children together, including Hattie Mae, Oprah's grandmother.

After Nelson died (sometime around 1907), Amanda married Charles Bullocks, also widowed, and had two children with him. Bullocks's mother was black and his father was white, and left a sizable amount of land to Charles. Bullocks's children from his previous marriage were very light skinned and they did not take to having a dark-skinned stepmother. They called her Black Mandy. Amanda, of course, deserved better. But these prejudices against dark skin were persistent. We can only imagine how being labeled in this manner must have pained her, in the same way that Oprah was pained by the color consciousness of Miss Miller.

Digging deeper, we discovered something truly remarkable about Amanda. When the NAACP was founded in the early twentieth century, one of its biggest supporters was a remarkably visionary and liberal philanthropist named Julius Rosenwald. Rosenwald had made a fortune with the Sears and Roebuck Company, and he was really passionate about what we would have called back then "Negro/white relations." Starting in 1912, he gave millions of dollars to help rural black communities set up elementary schools. Remarkably, in 1929, Oprah's great-grandmother Amanda became a trustee of one of these schools—a very rare feat for a woman of her day, white or black.

We first heard this story from Katharine Esters and were able

Oprah Winfrey's maternal great-grandmother, Amanda Presley Winters, with her second husband, Charles Bullocks, sometime after 1907. In 1929, Amanda became a trustee of the Buffalo Rosenwald School in Attala County, Mississippi—a rare accomplishment for a woman of her time, white or black. *From the personal collection of Katharine Carr Esters*

to verify it when we found a land deed in the state archives listing "Amanda Bullocks" (her name after she remarried) as one of the three trustees of the Buffalo Rosenwald School in Attala County, Mississippi. And in fact she was the school's sole woman trustee. How did she manage that? We can't be certain, but we discussed the question in detail with Mary Hoffschwelle, an excellent historian of the period, and she had several interesting thoughts on the matter.

"We know that women were critically important to any Rosenwald school building campaign," said Hoffschwelle. "Often, they were the leaders of the local fundraising campaign. But this is a little bit different. She's on the trustees board of her local school. That meant that she had responsibility for the maintenance of the school. She was one of the people helping to work with the superintendent on hiring the teacher for the school. And I think that the job of teacher is one of the keys here. Teachers were highly respected members of the community. They themselves were educated people. They were responsible then for the transmission of education to the next generation. When they became teachers, they realized their duties would not end in the classroom. So Amanda would not have thought of it as a duty being in that school classroom but as a responsibility to the community itself. And that meant a commitment to school improvement, making sure that the school in her community really met the needs of its students, helping to organize the community to maintain the school. It also meant that she was something of an authority figure already. Teachers were major authority figures, respected and sometimes seen as somebody to be not fearful of but to acknowledge their authority over you, and that too would have given her a measure of status."

Hoffschwelle felt that Amanda's status as a highly respected member of the church congregation might also have been a factor. "There were such close ties between schools and churches," Hoffschwelle reasoned, "that possibly her membership in the Buffalo Methodist church and her prominence within that church congregation also would have given reason for the community to see her as part of the trustees board and for the county superintendent to also see her as a logical member for that trustees board. After all, the church may well have been the sponsor for the original school and they were continuing that tradition on as well."

Finally, laughing, Hoffschwelle offered up a third possibility, perhaps considering that Amanda's line would lead eventually to the indomitable Oprah. "I would not discount the power of personality," said Hoffschwelle. "Amanda may just by sheer force of character and personality have been such a leader in the community that she would have been put onto the trustees board even though the initial way you would think about trustees is being male. Maybe she belonged there, as a community leader."

We tracked down plans and photographs of the Buffalo Rosenwald School in the Mississippi Department of Archives and History (in their collection of Rosenwald papers). We also discovered that finances for the school were broken down into $700 from the Rosenwald Fund, $300 from local white residents, and $2,650 from local black residents (which is impressive evidence of a commitment to education among the African American community—as this was at a time when, for every $1 the local authorities spent on white kids, they spent $0.07 on black kids!).

Katharine Esters was also able to tell us a good deal about the school, including some possible factors in Amanda's appointment. She claimed that there were very specific requirements that any candidate for the board of trustees of a Rosenwald School had to meet. For example, a candidate had to have a dictionary and other books in his or her home. So Amanda probably did. Furthermore, a candidate could not be encumbered with debt—and, indeed, Amanda owned her land debt-free thanks to her first husband, Nelson, who was a member of the Knights of Pythias, a Masonic order. Through that organization, Nelson had an insurance policy which stipulated that he could not borrow against his property. But other than these few details, we simply don't know how Amanda attained her position. I'm inclined to agree with Hoffschwelle's idea that her appointment was probably a sign of how powerful she was in her community. Regardless, however, even in the Civil Rights Era in the 1960s, women were often relegated to the back stage, to a second-class citizenship. For Amanda to be listed on this document in the early part of the twentieth century was quite extraordinary.

Amanda was clearly a very accomplished, able woman. According to Katharine Esters, she organized not only the school but also the United Methodist Church in Kosciusko. Yet her daughter, Hattie Mae Presley, Oprah's grandmother, grew up to be a semiliterate laundress. How did this happen? We don't know for sure, but we have some clues. Before she married Charles Bullocks, life for Amanda and her family was harsh. The 1910 census indicates that Amanda and all her children, including the ten-year-old Hattie Mae, were living on a farm and working as laborers. None of the children was attending school. Young Hattie Mae, the census indicates, could read but not write—and it's highly probable that her education was over at that point. She would be a laborer for the rest of her days.

We don't know when Amanda married Charles Bullocks, but it seems pretty clear that her circumstances improved after that marriage. Her children, however, may not have benefited much from Amanda's prosperity. Amanda became a school trustee in 1929. Hattie Mae was twenty-nine years old at the time—an adult whose formal education was well behind her. Charles and Amanda may have been unwilling or unable to assist her. It is also possible that Hattie Mae did not want assistance. We don't know.

The anecdote is fascinating to me, though, because it both vividly illustrates the precarious nature of progress and shows just how difficult the first four decades of the twentieth century were for poor rural Southerners, black and white. There were two major depressions and several minor ones and very few good economic years. (Hence the massive migration to the cities and to the North.) If you stayed in the South, as Hattie Mae and Amanda both did, you were extremely vulnerable economically. You didn't have much wealth and it was very difficult to preserve and pass on what you had. Even the bonds of family did not guarantee stability, as property and savings could be wiped away very quickly. Indeed, it is hardly surprising that Hattie Mae did not benefit significantly, if at all, from what seems to have been a period of prosperity in her mother's life—because the generation that came of age during the Great Depression by and large took a step backwards in the movement up the economic ladder that marks the story of so many American families. Hattie Mae was part of that generation and is strongly representative of it.

Amanda, too, was ultimately consumed by the larger economic forces of the time. She did not enjoy her prosperity for long. In fact, her ending was tragic. Records show that Amanda and her second husband, Charles Bullocks, borrowed money from the Federal Land Bank, and after he died, Amanda defaulted on payments and the bank seized the land. Although she offered to pay her debts with money from her children, the bank wanted the land because, according to Katharine, they didn't think it was right that a black man—and now, a black woman—had owned so much land. Three hundred acres was a tremendous amount of property. So the bank seized it, along with all of Amanda's belongings. She then moved to her first husband's land and lived in a shanty for the rest of her life, dying sometime around 1940.

Katharine remembers Amanda as a very dignified, no-nonsense person. In her earlier days, she would read storybooks to the children at family gatherings and entertain them. But later, when the bank foreclosed on her land, Katharine says Amanda was never the same person. She became quite sad and forlorn. She was always an especially disciplined person who "spoke the King's English." She spoke little of her parents and slavery other than to say that they would have rather died than lived as slaves.

Oprah was startled to learn that at the height of segregation, her great-grandmother was working to educate African Americans. "It feels like I've carried it on," she said. "It feels like she would be the kind of person you would have had to have been to be able to stand up in a room. I mean, I feel it myself now when I go into a corporate room and I'm the only black face in that room and I'm the only female. I often say that 'I come as one, but I stand as ten thousand,' which is a line from one of Maya [Angelou]'s poems."

I nodded my head in agreement as Oprah then told me something that could stand as the epigraph to all of my work in African American genealogy, naming something that I feel strongly about myself: "Before I have a big meeting or decision to make," she said, "I go and I sit with the ancestors. Literally, I go and I sit in my closet and I say their names. I just say their names and so that when I walk into the space, I don't walk alone. But I had no idea what she had done."

I feel that way every time I see my own family tree. "You come from people," my mother used to say to my brother and me, again and again. Like Oprah, I had no idea how deep these lines of our "people" would turn out to be.

Oprah is herself right now planning to build a school for young girls and young women—she's launching a huge boarding school in South Africa. So history is repeating itself. (Or, as Oprah says, the "psychic energy is being carried from generation to generation.") This is quite a coincidence. But, of course, environment is also one of the most likely predictors of a child's fate—we tend to occupy the same social class that our parents did. Although one can overcome this—and America is unique for its potential for social mobility—if you want to predict, basically, how a person is going to turn out, look at the social status of his or her parents.

That's why teenagers having babies are more likely to raise teenagers who have babies, too, than are members of other demographic groups. Unless an individual can overcome these odds, through sheer will and stubbornness and determination—or unless the larger society, through funding and implementing social mobility programs, such as Head Start or affirmative action, intervenes to break this cycle of the determining character of environment—environment will continue, all too often, to be destiny. The very history of the African American people, starting with the newly freed slaves, is a history of the hardheaded determination of a people to overcome their environment. I'm not the only African American of my generation who worries that a younger generation has forgotten this most basic aspect of the black tradition.

Oprah's maternal ancestors clearly shared her passion for education. And I wasn't the least bit surprised when I turned to the paternal side of her family tree and found another educator in her past. Her paternal great-grandfather—her father's grandfather—was Sanford Winfrey, born in 1872 in Poplar Creek, Mississippi, to Constantine and Violet Winfrey, both former slaves.

Much of what we learned about Sanford comes from oral history—especially from the testimony of his grandson Vernon, Oprah's father—and most of the stories matched against the public records. We know from the records, for example, that Sanford was married to Ella Staples, born in Choctaw County, Mississippi. (Ella's family can be traced forward to the Staples Singers, who are Oprah's distant cousins—indeed, one of Oprah's great-great-grandmothers on her father's side, Abigail Staples, is Mavis Staples's great-grandmother.)

Sanford and Ella had nine children and survived a terrible family tragedy. In 1931, Sanford's son, Vindee, killed his brother, Grover, in a dispute over Vindee's son, who wanted to live with Grover rather than his father. It was either premeditated murder or some kind of act of self-defense. But we can't be sure. We have newspaper articles and Grover's death certificate to support the fact of his death. We also know that Vindee was never convicted of the killing—court records indicate that his case ended after three mistrials, and he was never tried a fourth time. This may have been

An article from *The Winona Times* in Montgomery County, Mississippi, about Vindee Winfrey, the son of Oprah Winfrey's paternal great-grandfather, Sanford Winfrey. In 1931, Vindee killed his brother, Grover, in a dispute over Vindee's son, who wanted to live with Grover rather than with his father. Vindee was tried three times, but no jury was ever able to reach a verdict, and his case was ultimately dismissed.

Public Domain

NEGRO SHOT 9 TIMES BY HIS OWN BROTHER

Trouble Over The Custody Of A Child Resulted In The Killing—Negro In Jail.

Grover Winfrey, negro, age about 35, was shot and killed by his brother, C. C. Winfrey, 40, Saturday night. The killing occured in the highway near the Lavater Stoker place 'northeast of Winona.

Winfrey was shot nine times by his brother, six of the bullets from a 32 automatic taking effect. He died instantly.

The shooting is said to have been the outcome of a quarrel regarding the custody of a child.

Sheriff L. L. Latham went out to arrest the negro, but before he was located Paul Purnell, negro, took him in charge, later turning him over to the authorities. Winfrey is now in jail here.

reflective of Sanford's influence in the community, or, indeed, Vindee's lack of premeditation.

Beyond this, it was difficult to learn much about Sanford at first. His grandson Vernon hardly remembers him. "We would just see him once the year," says Vernon, "or a few times a year and we would go up for a visit on Sundays. Just for a few hours. And back in those days children played. They didn't allow you to hang around the grown folk and you didn't butt in grown people's conversations, so we never talked at length."

But as he continued to talk, it became clear that Vernon had learned a lot from listening to the stories of his older relatives. This is one of the great benefits of an oral history—as you explore a subject, people tend to open up and reveal reserves of knowledge they may not know they possess. "I heard my dad talk about Sanford," says Vernon. "He was the strict disciplinarian. And he was known to have been very stingy and tight with his money." Vernon then joked that Sanford helped start him on his way. "He gave me a dime once and I told him that I had been trying to add to it ever since," he said, laughing. Soon, a larger picture of the man began to emerge. I learned that Sanford was a well-respected gentleman. And he was a landowner. He died owning 200 acres of land in Poplar Creek, which he left to his heirs, and this land remains in the family today.

I also learned that Sanford was a farmer and may have been a teacher as well. Many towns in rural Mississippi had a one-room schoolhouse for black children. Vernon claimed that Sanford was the head teacher and that he taught all subjects through all ages. Friends and neighbors even called him "the Professor." According to Vernon, even Sanford's wife had to call him this—"I heard my daddy say his wife had to call him Professor Winfrey or Mr. Winfrey." We might say, today, that Sanford was one bad dude!

We couldn't find a record of Sanford being paid to teach, so we cannot confirm Vernon's claim that his grandfather was a teacher. Nonetheless, Vernon has many memories of that small schoolhouse, which offer a vivid portrait of education for blacks in rural Mississippi at the time. "Back in those days," he says, "it was just one teacher in one little shack. And I remember one teacher in particular, while she taught this class you sat over there and you stayed quiet. If not she kept a switch about so long. And she would use it. And if you got a whipping at school, you would be in the hopes that your parents didn't find out about it. If they found out, you got another whipping. You were corrected by everybody. Any adult that you passed on the way to school, if they saw that any children were out of order or playing too long? They might tell our mother or daddy."

Vernon was also able to evoke a sense of the importance that education played in his family's life. He says that his father, Elmore, often spoke of how his grandfather Sanford insisted that his children learn to read and write—and that Elmore often reminded him proudly that two of his sisters became schoolteachers. Both his grandfather and his father seemed to be preaching to him constantly about the role of education. "I didn't realize the importance of it when I was young, coming up," he said, "but I learned later in life when I got out on my own that I should have listened to my father and have grasped it more than I did."

Education, education, education. It's remarkable to me, as I review Oprah's family history, how many of her ancestors were involved in education! If Oprah Winfrey's life and ancestry share a motif, it is this: that education can set you free, even if you're black, illiterate, and an ex-slave. Oprah has a deep, almost intuitive understanding of the crucial importance of education to our people, and, indeed, to us all: "Education is freedom," she says, "like an open door. And it's colorblind." I feel the same way. I have long known that education is a tool—a tool that has been uniquely important to blacks since they were first brought to America. I have always been fascinated by this aspect of our history. Trying to understand it better, we spoke to Leslie Rowland, a fellow historian. We asked her what conditions were like for blacks who wanted an education in the late nineteenth century.

"They had few resources," says Rowland, "and the fact that they were so impoverished makes it all the more impressive, the enormous commitments that they made to education. In many parts of the South, free people held mass meetings in which they agreed to tax themselves to support schools. Many free people paid tuition for their children's education. A great deal of labor in kind was contributed to schools. They would build the school. They made the tables and benches for the schools. Freed people in the neighborhood provided room and board to teachers. The northern teachers who were in the South often commented on the number of gifts that freed people dropped off for them: eggs, cakes, etc. Freed people did everything they could to support their schools. Often, because they had little money, what they gave was their time and labor."

Of course, in establishing schools, African Americans like Oprah's great-grandparents encountered daunting obstacles. One was their impoverished condition. Another was the pervasive racial violence of their age. Blacks who sought an education faced terrible danger, even during Reconstruction, that period when so much hope seemed alive, when genuine freedom and social mobility appeared attainable, after the long dark night of slavery. Literacy was always slavery's greatest threat, the most profound threat to the status quo. It still is, in fact. "Free men," says Rowland, "often formed companies that would guard the schools at night because the schools were always subject to attack by white neighbors who did not welcome a black school. The opposition of local whites ranged from white children who would throw stones at black children to attacks at night, arson. Hundreds of black schools were burned in the Reconstruction

Era. In the Memphis Riot of 1866, for example, black schools and black churches were targeted and most were destroyed."

And yet African Americans persisted in demanding education. And over time, they succeeded. "Freed people contributed to education by letting their churches be used as schools," says Rowland. "Often the first school was held in whatever black church was available."

Other obstacles included the difficulty of finding teachers. "Since there were so few freed people who were literate," says Rowland, "they welcomed with open arms the teachers who came from northern aid societies, but they also quickly tried to prepare themselves to become teachers. And the generation of freed people who were the students in the schools of Reconstruction became the foundation of the teacher corps that would populate the black schools, particularly after Reconstruction when funding was diminished. These teachers who had been taught in those early schools provided the backbone. Most of the northern teachers were gone after about 1870."

So those first students in the Reconstruction Era became the teachers of the next generation—and Oprah's ancestors were among them. Indeed, they were leading their sisters and brothers along the way, cutting a path through the densest of forests, unlighted. It was a bold journey on which they embarked, like pioneers and explorers attempting to navigate their way through the darkest, uncharted waters. But these people—Oprah's ancestors and people like them—are heroes of the African American tradition just as surely as are Sojourner Truth and Frederick Douglass, Rosa Parks and the Reverend Dr. Martin Luther King, Jr. We fail to remember and honor the contributions of public school teachers to African American history, especially in the turbulent early days of freedom, at our peril.

PART FOUR

Out of Slavery:
A Paper Trail

I wrote in the previous chapter about the panic I felt when I learned that many of the records related to Oprah's ancestors had been destroyed in various fires and natural disasters. That panic was real—and it afflicts every genealogist and every historian. Those kinds of records are simply invaluable to anyone who wants to reconstruct a family tree. Birth certificates, marriage licenses, land deeds—these sorts of documents set down mundane, everyday aspects of any citizen's life. You need them if you want to trace your family back through time. They are also, I have learned doing these documentaries for PBS, remarkably instructive even to a scholar of African American history. By examining the records of Oprah's ancestors, I learned a tremendous amount about the larger experience of African Americans in this country, things that you'll rarely, if ever, read in history books because they are seemingly so specific, so "minor," so "trivial," so inextricably intertwined with the particularity of one individual's daily existence. But taken together, stories such as these are quite powerful, and sometimes can even alter the shape of the broader history of our people.

For obvious reasons, historians need to generalize about large patterns of behavior or treatment, rather than dwell on the uniqueness of one family's story line. Not so with genealogy. Indeed, one of the great pleasures I take in genealogy is that it is almost the opposite of historical analysis in one significant way: Genealogy is all about the specific, the trivial details in one family's life, regardless of how these details fit, or accord, with larger historical trends or generalities. Genealogy is all about what made your ancestors tick, what they did with their lives, and how they did these things, not what they should have done or were "supposed" to do, even if what happened to them was exceptional. And therein lies its great value, as I see it. If we can begin to understand what made our ancestors tick, we might be able to understand what made their contemporaries tick, and, ultimately, what makes ourselves tick.

A wealth of seemingly trivial facts pertaining to Oprah's family that we found in the local newspapers and historical documents helped me to understand how her grandfather Elmore achieved such a respected place in the black community in Kosciusko, Mississippi. I learned, for example, that between 1890 and 1900, Kosciusko's population grew 60 percent because new factories were built. Thus, despite my sense that Oprah's family lived through years of subsistence farming and, sometimes, crushing poverty, there is some evidence of economic mobility in their environment, of which, perhaps, they were able to take advantage. For a time, Kosciusko was growing wealthier. There was even a housing shortage at one point. In 1930, when there were 1,952 black farmers in Attala County, it was estimated that 10 percent of them, or approximately two hundred, owned their own farms. The average black farm was 60 acres, but a few were larger. Elmore's farm, purchased in nearby Carroll County in 1942, was much larger—104 acres—which helps to explain why he had such prominence in his community. In fact, Elmore eventually moved to Kosciusko, where on December 12, 1956, he leased land (less than an acre) on North Natchez Street for $2,850, which he paid "cash in hand." To have accumulated this much savings was a remarkable achievement for a black person in the South, especially if we recall that this transaction occurred just a year after the Montgomery Bus Boycott, in neighboring Alabama, began.

I also learned that Kosciusko was the first town in Attala County to establish a separate school district from the rest of the county; it was divided into twelve grades and observed a school term of seven months rather than the more traditional four. I learned that in August 1877, a state teachers association was formed. There were thirty-four teachers, and, incredibly, four of those were colored. The salary for a first-grade teacher in 1875 was $55.47 per month. But by 1885, pay had dropped to $28.74 per month, starting a trend in the underfunding of public education in Mississippi that continues today.

Such things are fascinating to me because they give a sense of the forces and factors that shaped people's lives—the things that may have influenced Sanford and his son, Elmore, to stay in the brutal Jim Crow South, just as almost 133,000 Free Negroes had, stunningly, remained in the Confederacy during the length of the Civil War. (A total of 250,000 Free Negroes lived in the Confederate states and the slaveholding Border States combined.)

But records like these can only take you back so far into the past; they cannot readily take us back into slavery. Slavery poses enormous challenges to genealogists searching for black roots. Names, records, family structures—all were intentionally repressed by the slave owners. For the genealogist, perhaps the most complicated aspect of slavery is one of the simplest practices—the naming of the individual slaves. In 1865, when the Civil War ended, most of our ancestors had only one name: a first name. That's what the slavery system did: It took away our ancestors' names, took away their identities. And it did this systematically, perversely.

This erasure was completely and cruelly intended, of course. It was a primary part of the system of bondage, religiously recording the slaves' existence as property, but just as religiously denying them human agency, denying them their status as human beings. Slaveholders, although they knew better, couldn't even intimate to their slaves that they realized how human they were, that they were just as human as any white woman or white man. Accordingly, legal records of slaves all share a common lie, i.e., these "beings" are not traceable by name, because they are not human beings. To the own-

1860 Federal Census Summary
Figures summarized from: http://www2.census.gov/prod2/decennial/documents/18601-15.pdf

All States:	Total Free Population	Total Free Colored	Total Indians	Total Slaves	Total Population	Total Population	Percent of Total Population				
							Percent Free Colored	Percent Indian	Percent Slaves	Percent White	
ALABAMA	529,121	2,690	160	435,080		964,201	0.28%	0.02%	45.12%	54.58%
ARKANSAS	324,335	144	48	111,115		435,450	0.03%	0.01%	25.52%	74.44%
CALIFORNIA	379,994	4,086	17,798			379,994	1.08%	4.68%	0.00%	94.24%
COLORADO	34,277	46				34,277	0.13%	0.00%	0.00%	99.87%
CONNECTICUT	460,147	8,627	16			460,147	1.87%	0.00%	0.00%	98.12%
DAKOTA	4,837		2,261			4,837	0.00%	46.74%	0.00%	53.26%
DELAWARE	110,418	19,829		1,798		112,216	17.67%	0.00%	1.60%	80.73%
DIST. OF COLUMBIA	71,895	11,131	1	3,185		75,080	14.83%	0.00%	4.24%	80.93%
FLORIDA	78,679	932		61,745		140,424	0.66%	0.00%	43.97%	55.37%
GEORGIA	595,088	3,500	38	462,198		1,057,286	0.33%	0.00%	43.72%	55.95%
ILLINOIS	1,711,951	7,628	32			1,711,951	0.45%	0.00%	0.00%	99.55%
INDIANA	1,350,428	11,428	290			1,350,428	0.85%	0.02%	0.00%	99.13%
IOWA	674,913	1,069	65			674,913	0.16%	0.01%	0.00%	99.83%
KANSAS (territory)	107,204	625	189	2		107,206	0.58%	0.18%	0.00%	99.24%
KENTUCKY	930,201	10,684	33	225,483		1,155,684	0.92%	0.00%	19.51%	79.56%
LOUISIANA	376,276	18,647	173	331,726		708,002	2.63%	0.02%	46.85%	50.49%
MAINE	628,279	1,327	5			628,279	0.21%	0.00%	0.00%	99.79%
MARYLAND	599,860	83,942		87,189		687,049	12.22%	0.00%	12.69%	75.09%
MASSACHUSETTS	1,231,066	9,602	32			1,231,066	0.78%	0.00%	0.00%	99.22%
MICHIGAN	749,113	6,799	6,172			749,113	0.91%	0.82%	0.00%	98.27%
MINNESOTA	172,023	259	2,369			172,023	0.15%	1.38%	0.00%	98.47%
MISSISSIPPI	354,674	773	2	436,631		791,305	0.10%	0.00%	55.18%	44.72%
MISSOURI	1,067,081	3,572	20	114,931		1,182,012	0.30%	0.00%	9.72%	89.97%
NEBRASKA (territory)	28,826	67	63	15		28,841	0.23%	0.22%	0.05%	99.50%
NEVADA (territory)	6,857	45				6,857	0.66%	0.00%	0.00%	99.34%

1860 Federal Census Summary
Figures summarized from: http://www2.census.gov/prod2/decennial/documents/18601-15.pdf

All States:	Total Free Population	Total Free Colored	Total Indians	Total Slaves	Total Population	Percent of Total Population			
						Percent Free Colored	Percent Indian	Percent Slaves	Percent White
NEW HAMPSHIRE	326,073	494			326,073	0.15%	0.00%	0.00%	99.85%
NEW JERSEY	672,017	25,318		18	672,035	3.77%	0.00%	0.00%	96.23%
NEW MEXICO	93,516	85	10,507		93,516	0.09%	11.24%	0.00%	88.67%
NEW YORK	3,880,735	49,005	140		3,880,735	1.26%	0.00%	0.00%	98.73%
NORTH CAROLINA	661,563	30,463	1,158	331,059	992,622	3.07%	0.12%	33.35%	63.46%
OHIO	2,339,511	36,673	30		2,339,511	1.57%	0.00%	0.00%	98.43%
OREGON	52,465	128	177		52,465	0.24%	0.34%	0.00%	99.42%
PENNSYLVANIA	2,906,215	56,949	7		2,906,215	1.96%	0.00%	0.00%	98.04%
RHODE ISLAND	174,620	3,952	19		174,620	2.26%	0.01%	0.00%	97.73%
SOUTH CAROLINA	301,302	9,914	88	402,406	703,708	1.41%	0.01%	57.18%	41.40%
TENNESSEE	834,082	7,300	60	275,719	1,109,801	0.66%	0.01%	24.84%	74.49%
TEXAS	421,649	355	403	182,566	604,215	0.06%	0.07%	30.22%	69.66%
UTAH	40,244	30	80	29	40,273	0.07%	0.20%	0.07%	99.65%
VERMONT	315,098	709	20		315,098	0.23%	0.01%	0.00%	99.77%
VIRGINIA	1,105,453	58,042	112	490,865	1,596,318	3.64%	0.01%	30.75%	65.61%
WASHINGTON	11,594	30	426		11,594	0.26%	3.67%	0.00%	96.07%
WISCONSIN	775,881	1,171	613		775,881	0.15%	0.08%	0.00%	99.77%
Totals	27,489,561	488,070	43,607	3,953,760	31,443,321	1.55%	0.14%	12.57%	85.73%

A chart created by the genealogist Jane Ailes, using data from the 1860 federal census. The chart indicates the number of whites, slaves, free blacks, and Indians in each state just before the Civil War. It provides a useful glimpse of America's racial composition at that time. *From the personal collection of Jane Ailes*

ers, they were things; they were property, listed in tax records along with the chickens, the horses, and the cows, for example. The records that do exist merely count them and list them, sometimes by gender and age, sometimes by skin color, almost never by name.

Marriages were forbidden. Though many slaves entered into more or less permanent relations (some of which were formalized after the Civil War), these were not recognized by white masters or their laws—and they thus generated no records. They were informal. Deaths, too, were of no consequence—except to the bottom line of the plantation owners. The passing of a slave may have posed a financial burden, but it did not generate a death certificate. Religion was encouraged to make slaves submissive, but literacy was outlawed, so black churches could keep no records of who attended their services.

There were rare exceptions to these practices, however. For example, some white Baptist and Presbyterian churches kept records of black members of their congregations, even those who were still slaves. Jane Ailes found an instance in Allegany County, Maryland, where a slave owner took his slaves to the local Catholic church to have them married by a priest. These marriages were recorded in the church's records. In the 1850 and 1860 U.S. federal census, mortality schedules include the names of slaves—generally by first name—who had died in the twelve months before the census was taken. In Hardy County, Virginia, the deaths of slaves are recorded among the general death records. But for the vast majority of slaves, there is no documentary record.

How can we get past these bizarre, racist conventions when we go about the business of reconstructing our family trees? By understanding our history and knowing what kind of documents we *can* look for. By understanding what slavery was—how it worked to reinforce, psychologically, our ancestors' legal status as objects, as property, as subhuman beings ostensibly of a different order completely than fully human whites.

There are all kinds of examples of this. Famously, the abolitionist Sojourner Truth, while a slave in New York, experienced the horror of learning that her small son had been given as a wedding present to the master's daughter. Truth came home one day and found out her son had been shipped to the Deep South. Just try to imagine that! And realize that if the son had stayed in New York, he would have been freed as New York's gradual emancipation law played itself out. But he was gone. And Sojourner Truth had virtually no recourse.

The sense of dislocation and discontinuity in the African American community must have been enormous. As the historian James Horton explains it: "As the South expands into the Southwest, into what we call the Deep South—that region of Louisiana and Mississippi and Alabama that's just hungry for slaves—well, suddenly you can buy a slave in the upper South, in Virginia, for a few hundred dollars and sell them for a few thousand dollars in New Orleans. And lots and lots of working-class whites who couldn't afford to be planters made lots of money as slave traders. That provided a situation in which young males, strong and healthy, were transported from the Upper South to work on the large plantations of the Lower South. And that process tore black families apart, because what that means is that somebody's son, somebody's father, somebody's brother is being sold away to the Lower South. Now there were some women who were taken South as well and some children even, but the largest proportion were young adult males. And so what you get, starting really in the early part of the nineteenth century, is the breaking apart of families."

The deconstruction of the black family was one of the most pernicious by-products of the slavery system, a tragedy that has echoed throughout black America ever since. At the end of the Civil War, four million African Americans were finally freed from bondage. Free——in theory, at least——to take charge of their own lives: to buy property, to get an education, to reunite their families. Among them were my Gates and Coleman ancestors, and Oprah Winfrey's ancestors. Flash forward a century, and we are still dealing with the trauma and discontinuity of their lives. Oprah and I, like most African Americans, know next to nothing about our ancestors who were enslaved.

I think that it's almost impossible for us to grasp how severe, how comprehensive, was this attempt to obliterate the humanity of African human beings who were sold into slavery in this country. And yet, if this is so, then how in the world are we to learn about the lives of our enslaved ancestors? How are we to glimpse these women and men whom the American society attempted to render invisible in the written records any sophisticated society must keep to preserve and maintain order, especially its legacy of property rights and entitlements?

It is very difficult to find one's ancestors who were enslaved, to locate their identities in any written record created before 1870, when the first federal census included all of the African American people——former slaves as well as those who had managed, somehow, to gain their freedom before the Civil War, which ended in 1865——by first and last names for the very first time! It's difficult, but it's not impossible. In fact, if you're able to trace your family back to the 1870 census, chances are that you will be able to identify an additional generation of your ancestors——as well as the names of the white people who owned them, provided your ancestors took as their surname the name of the white people who owned them, and if they didn't leave the county where they'd been enslaved, as recently even as 1860. Let me explain how you go about doing this.

While historians debate the precise statistics, the consensus among most scholars is that a majority of slaves took the surnames of their masters upon gaining their freedom. Because this fact is so very crucial to identifying one's black ancestors during slavery— just as we did, as you'll see, with Oprah's ancestors—it's worth pausing to examine the evidence for this important claim (though I shall return to discuss this again, later in this chapter). Elizabeth Shown Mills, a genealogist, in a study published in 1986, had this to say about her results: "A sample study made by the present writer, from 696 ex-slave testimonies given before the three Civil War commissions," taken between 1871 and 1884, "indicates that in seventy-one percent of the cases, the ex-slave used the surname of the man whom he identified as his last master; two percent reverted to using the name of an earlier master; and twenty-five percent did not use the name of any identifiable owner. In a small number of cases (two percent)," she concludes, "no names of former masters could be determined and the origins of the slaves' names were unquantifiable." Mills's results were for slaves from Alabama and Louisiana, in the two decades immediately following emancipation.

The historian Melvin Collier, on the other hand, examining the names that ex-slaves were using when they were interviewed as late as the 1930s by the WPA, found that of 135 former slaves (a much smaller sample than Mills examined) from Mississippi and Arkansas, 43.2 percent from Mississippi were still using the same surname as their last slave master, while in Arkansas only 18.5 percent were. (Similarly, the historian Herbert Gutman found that 27 percent, 49 of 181, of former slaves from North Carolina were using their master's surname in the 1930s, while roughly 34 percent, 74 of 217, were also doing so in Texas at the same time, some seventy years after slavery. It's quite likely that some slaves changed their surnames the further in time they were removed from slavery.)

Given the difference in the sizes of the samples among these studies, and given that Mills's study was of slaves who had been recently freed, her study is the most relevant of the three for those of us searching for our slave ancestors through the 1870 federal census. In other words, if you are fortunate enough to find your ancestor in the 1870 census, there is a strong probability that if you look at the 1860 federal census for a white slaveholder with the same surname, living in the same or a nearby county as your ancestor was living in 1870, your ancestor may have been the property of that person, or of one of his or her relatives.

(There are exceptions to this general principle: In my own family, for example, a white slave owner named Abraham Vanmeter freed Joe and Sarah Bruce—my fourth great-grandfather and -grandmother, on my mother's side—and their children in 1823. Vanmeter and his wife, Elizabeth, gave them hundreds of acres of land, a grist mill, a house, livestock, cash, and all the household goods. Nevertheless, the former slaves did not take the surname Vanmeter; they used the surname of Bruce. Another family freed by the Vanmeters used the name of Grey. And while we have theories about this, we still are not sure why! So we must be careful not to presume a relationship simply because of a similarity in surnames. On the other hand, the odds are strongly in favor that a black family named Bruce, for example, took that name at some point from a white family named Bruce who owned them, even if we don't know when. This assumption—and it is only an assumption—is quite useful as you start your journey into your ancestors' slave past, even if you must use it cautiously.)

This matter of the names that slaves called themselves, both before the Civil War and immediately following it, is very important and complex. And to make matters even more interesting, consider these anomalies, as Jane Ailes reports: "Occasionally," she told me, "a slave was enumerated by surname in the general population schedule of the federal census. These were households 'living out,' which meant that the slaves were living independently of their master, in their own households. One example is Robert B. Bolling, listed in the federal census of 1840, in Dinwiddie County, Virginia. The census taker noted in Bolling's case that 'no white person resides.'" A few more slaves, also "living out," are listed in the same county, along with Bolling, also by their surnames.

While the United States census did not list the slaves by name prior to the Civil War, in 1850 the federal government created what were called slave schedules, in which our ancestors were recorded as nameless objects of property. These schedules also provide, in the rarest of cases, a few other opportunities for discovering the first, or given, names of a small number of slaves. For example, Ailes notes, "In three slaveholding counties throughout the United States in the 1850 census—including Utah County, Utah; Bowie County, Texas; and Scott County, Tennessee—and five slaveholding counties in the 1860 census—including Boyde County, Kentucky; Camden County, North Carolina; Washington County, Tennessee (Districts Nine and Seventeen); the City of St. Louis, Missouri (in the Second Ward only); and in Hampshire County, Virginia [where my ancestors lived]—the census slave schedules contain the first names of the slaves." This is quite remarkable, and is very promising, if your ancestors happen to have lived in one of these eight counties in either 1850 or 1860.

One other anomaly is of equal interest: If a slave was older than one hundred years, the census taker was to note their name in the schedule. "And occasionally," Ailes concludes, "the census mortality schedules for 1850 and 1860 note the names of slaves, and usually the name of the deceased's owner, who died within the preceding year." With these very rare exceptions, however, the slaves listed in the slave schedules were anonymous, their names erased by the attempt to dehumanize a person, to turn a woman or man into a thing.

With all this in mind, and even noting the exceptions, the best way to commence your efforts to penetrate what I think of as "The Document Void of Enslavement"—to begin to force the Abyss of Slavery to speak our ancestors' names—is by looking for the names of ancestors who survived the Civil War and lived as free men and women and were recorded in the 1870 federal census.

Whenever I look at the 1870 census, I feel as if I'm witnessing the birth of an entire people—at least the birth of a people through the Adamic function of naming. Why? Because this is the first census in which African Americans are uniformly listed with first and last names, the same as white people had been for decades. (The first federal census was taken in 1790, but included only "heads of households," which the census continued to list exclusively until 1850.) Imagine what it must have felt like to be able to claim your own first and last name for the first time before the law. How exhilarating that must have been! It must have been like being reborn, born again as a citizen.

This census is invaluable to genealogists. After freedom came, many African Americans looked for family members who'd been sold away. People placed ads in newspapers or read notices in black churches. These can be found in the archives of historical societies and libraries across the South—but be prepared to spend a great deal of effort to locate them. It's far easier to begin the search for your ancestors who survived slavery by turning to the census records, especially from 1870. There are also many different kinds of government records. These are a bit easier to track down, but the census records are especially informative.

Except in a few extraordinary cases, as we've seen, prior to the Civil War, the U.S. census didn't list African slaves by name. Nevertheless, in 1850, the federal government created the slave schedules wherein our ancestors were recorded as property, like cows, sheep, and goats. The genealogist Johni Cerny explains this all very clearly. "In those days," she told me, "the federal government didn't just come around and count heads. They had three or four different schedules that were attached to the census. They had what was called the population schedule, which was the head count of free people, white, black, and Indian. And they had a separate slave schedule that counted the slaves. That was tied into voting. In slave states, a master's slaves counted toward the electoral votes and the representation that those states had. So even though the slaves themselves couldn't vote, they got counted—so that their owners' representation was enhanced." The crazy psychotic injustice of that never ceases to amaze me. But these schedules are very useful to genealogists. They don't list the slaves by name, because they were property, but they do list them by gender, color, and age.

Why is this important? What good is it if you see listed in the 1850 census a slave identified as "black" in color (rather than mulatto), "twenty-seven years old," and a "male," with no name? Well, the slave schedules are organized by the name of the white person who owned these slaves. If one of your ancestors, let's say, called himself "Winfrey" for his last name in the 1870 census, it might be useful to look in the 1860 slave schedule in the same county for a white Winfrey who may have owned slaves. And if your Winfrey ancestor, again in 1870, is listed as "black" and a "male," aged "forty-seven," there is a reasonable possibility that the slave listed as twenty-seven in 1850 living on the Winfrey plantation is the same individual! Using this technique, we can sometimes find the identities of slaves whom the legal system sought to keep anonymous, or unnamed. But don't rely solely upon this type of information be-

cause it can be misleading. Continue to pursue other avenues of research to verify the slave owner's identity.

Another especially rich source of information about our enslaved ancestors are the wills and estate papers of the slaves' owners. Let's say that a slave's master died. His or her estate would be
inventoried and appraised. Later, these assets would be distributed
to the heirs. The estate inventory and appraisal documents will
name, item by item, even—or especially, because they were so
valuable—each of the deceased person's slaves. In this list the slaves
are usually named and their ages are often given. The slave owner,
often listing each slave by name in the will, would record his wishes
about how the slaves were to be distributed to heirs. You'll find
these estate papers recorded in the county courthouse where the
slave owner resided. They are a treasure trove of information for
genealogical research.

A third source for this kind of information are the records
generated by the Freedmen's Bureau, which was created by Congress in March 1865 to oversee the transition of African Americans
from slavery to freedom. Although it was initially established to be
a short-term agency, the bureau maintained offices throughout the
South for almost seven years. During that time, its agents were
charged with overseeing labor contracts and dealing with the
everyday problems of the former slaves, addressing everything
from food shortages to educational needs. Over time, the agents
also took on the role of hearing judicial disputes.

In this period, black testimony was not accepted in the state
courts, so freed black people could take their problems to the
Freedmen's Bureau agents instead. Though their efforts were
largely ineffective and almost completely obliterated by Jim Crow
segregationists once Reconstruction was abandoned in 1876, many
bureau agents were Northerners who were sympathetic to the

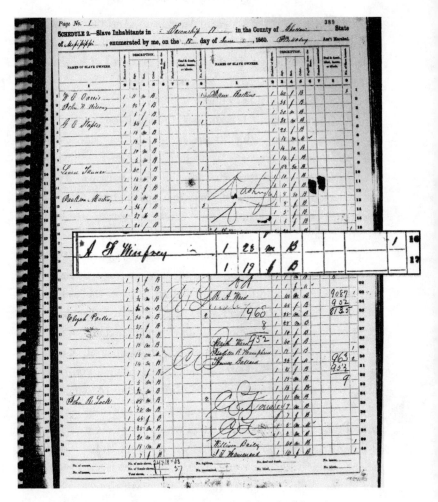

An 1860 Choctaw County, Mississippi, Slave Schedule, which lists slave owners on the left column and their slaves on the right, noting age, gender, and skin color of each slave. The slave owner Absalom Winfrey is listed as "A. F. Winfrey" on the sixteenth line of the right-hand column of slave owners. He is the owner of seven slaves, quite probably including Constantine, age twenty-three, and Violet, age nineteen. Constantine and Violet are Oprah Winfrey's paternal great-great-grandparents. *Public Domain*

plight of the newly freed African Americans. And they generated a wealth of paperwork that paints a vivid picture of life during Reconstruction for the ex-slaves who endured it, all of which can be accessed through the U.S. National Archives. (Many of these records are now available online.)

Taken together, the Freedmen's Bureau's records and the 1870 census data—combined with the pre–Civil War slave schedules and estate division records as well as newspaper archives—can provide a great deal of information that may help you trace your family back into slavery. But a warning is needed here. Genealogical research is so time-consuming and can be so very frustrating, that each of us has a tendency toward wishful thinking; we turn assumptions into facts, and will seize on an apparent similarity in name or coincidence of association to make the most outrageous claims. My own family did this in the case of Horatio Gates, the well-known general in the Revolutionary War. After years of searching, there does not seem to be a single shred of evidence that any of the black Gateses from whom I'm descended had anything at all in common with the good General Gates, other than sharing a common surname. But I still can't convince one of my cousins of that!

Especially troubling in this regard is the relationship between common last names of a slave and a white family. As we have seen, all too often we simply assume that when slavery ended, slaves took the last names of their masters. And, statistically, this is a reasonable assumption, judging from Elizabeth Shown Mills's research, which I cited earlier. But this fascinating subject is hotly debated among genealogists and historians.

Among the scholars with whom I have consulted, there is some disagreement over how strongly one can make the link between slave and slave owner solely based on matching surnames and close proximity of residence soon after emancipation. Some genealogists tend to be overly reliant on this assumption, while some cast doubt on it. One individual has even told me that slaves very *rarely* took their most recent slave owner's last name—which, based on my reading of the scholarship on this subject, especially Mills's research, and my own experience, I don't believe is true. On the other hand, the great educator Booker T. Washington wrote famously in his autobiography, *Up From Slavery,* that one of the things most newly freed slaves did was walk off the plantation where they'd been held as slaves (even if they just turned around and returned to become sharecroppers!), and in some way changed their names (even if such a name change involved only adding a middle initial, which, Washington says, the slaves thought of as one of the "entitlements" of freedom). Even if they didn't have a middle name, the initial was a meaningful statement about their new identity. So although I have seen enough concrete evidence of the taking of a former master's last name to think that "very rarely" is an exaggeration, I realize that the researcher offering that assessment has done most of her work in Virginia, which might differ in this respect from the more southern states. In fact, several of my own ancestors from Virginia, such as the Bruces, conform to this practice of taking the name of a master once-removed, as it were, rather than of their last owner. The location of one's ancestors who were slaves is of some importance to this matter.

The entire subject is very compelling, I think. And it is central to finding your slave ancestors through the records of the people who owned them. Moreover, naming is such a crucial part of the African American experience. I turned to my friend Ira Berlin, one of the preeminent scholars of slavery, to ask him his thoughts on this. Specifically, I was curious as to whether there have been any studies done noting the geographical differences between former slaves who took their master's names and those who didn't—in other words, studies comparing the results found by scholars such as Elizabeth Shown Mills and Melvin Collier, both cited earlier.

"This business of naming," Berlin said, "is interesting and extremely telling. Do not presume a link between the name of slave and name of slave owners. Doing so can be quite misleading, in fact. For example a letter exists from a Freedmen's Bureau agent in 1865 who reported that newly freed slaves in his district were purposely taking names other than their owners' because they feared that they would be re-enslaved (not an irrational fear if you surmise that if white men could enslave and then free, they might enslave again) and they would be once again attached to their old owners. Taking a different name would at least slow the process. But that is just one instance. The patterns are complicated and differ in place and time. I am afraid there is no one book on the subject, and much that is known is gleaned from small shards of evidence like the above. Even when black people did take the names of their owners, it was often not the name of their last owner. Often they tried to reach back in time to establish a family line."

We discussed this issue with historian Leslie Rowland. "As ex-slaves reunited their families and put their families on legal standing," she said, "one of the things that emerged was their family names, their surnames. The records we have show that most slaves during slavery mostly use only their given names, their first names. But in the records in the postwar period, people all had surnames. And the common supposition is that they took the surnames of their owners and in some cases that was true. But many, many freed people revealed to the world for the first time surnames that they may have used some time among themselves. One black soldier testifying at a court martial, when questioned about the surname he was using—why it wasn't the same as his owner's—responded: 'Well it was my father's name.' And the questioner said: 'Well where did your father get it?' He said it was his father's name."

Many slaves had family names that may not have been known to their owners at all, and with freedom those names emerged. They were sort of underground names, secret names, names that had necessarily been hidden from their white owners, which they used among themselves, no doubt, but which only surfaced following slavery, like a coded, submerged naming system. Quietly keeping surnames was also a way for slaves to maintain dignity and keep track of family ties in spite of slavery's oppressive practice of fracturing families. Sometimes, official documents noted the surnames that the slaves called themselves, perhaps as a sign of respect. Still other former slaves, seeking to make an entirely new start as freed people, made up their own last names, out of whole cloth.

Rowland explained the impulse to adopt a new surname: "Some ex-slaves clearly took new names. This was an opportunity to take new surnames. Particularly striking to me is the number of Freemans who appear on lists. Daniel Freeman, George Freeman. This was a choice of a name that signaled one's new status. Many of the other surnames that show up on the records of ex-slaves are prominent names, like Washington, Jefferson. And so it's thought that perhaps this was a way to connect oneself with power—through some powerful names. Often the family names used by slaves may have been the surname of some very distant owner, perhaps the owner of someone several generations back. But throughout the South, you can see this proliferation of names as people revealed names previously hidden and selected new names for themselves."

As you can tell—judging from the amount of time I've spent discussing it—I'm endlessly fascinated by this subject of the names the slaves took, both before and after slavery. But don't allow the issue's complexities to overwhelm you as you research your family tree. Reasonable assumptions can be made, especially if you understand the issues involved, and if you're willing to do the research necessary to back up your assumptions. It's not an easy task. But few tasks are more important. Discoveries of this sort are enormously exciting, and fruitful. Indeed, one thing I've learned from making documentaries about African American ancestry is that nothing, not even learning the name of the tribe from which one or two of our ancestors was descended in Africa—not even resolving that deep and abiding mystery—is as moving to most African Americans as identifying the names of ancestors who were enslaved in the early part of the nineteenth century, people born in the earliest decades of the 1800s. I tend to think of this as genealogical resurrection: reconstructing the identities of ancestors long thought anonymous, irretrievable, ancestors whom we had presumed to be long dead and gone forever.

After researching Oprah's family back more than three generations, I came to that great abyss in our shared history: the void of slavery wherein the overwhelming percentage of our ancestors cease to exist as human beings, much less citizens, and indeed have no names that the legal system was bound to honor or acknowledge. They were just property, plain and simple.

To overcome this, we followed many of the steps outlined above, starting out by turning to the 1870 U.S. census—the first U.S. census, as we have seen, that listed African Americans with two names, first and last. This census is so very important in black genealogy. It is the line that, metaphorically, separates B.C. from A.D. And it yielded information that proved invaluable in tracking down Oprah's slave ancestors.

Looking back along Oprah's maternal line from her grandparents, we focused on Earlist Lee and Hattie Mae Presley and began our journey back into the slave period. Earlist's parents were Harold and Elizabeth Lee. According to the 1870 census,

Harold was born a slave about 1855 in Hinds County, Mississippi. Earlist's mother, Elizabeth, was also born in Mississippi, sometime around 1875. So Harold was a former slave and Elizabeth was not. And going back another generation, we found Grace and John Lee, Harold's parents—also listed in the 1870 census. Now these are Oprah's great-great-grandparents, and they were both born in Mississippi in 1833. They were slaves for the first thirty-two years of their lives. And for an historian this is where it gets interesting. If black people didn't have names, two names, legally, until 1870, how in the world do we know that Grace and John Lee were born in 1833, and that these are Oprah Winfrey's great-great-grandparents?

To find out any information about John and Grace Lee, we had to look for records of white slave owners in this region using the slave schedules. So we looked for slave owners in Mississippi named Lee and we found the 1860 slave schedule for someone called S.E. Lee. And it shows that S.E. Lee owned a female slave, aged twenty-six, which is how old Oprah's great-great-grandmother, Grace, would've been in 1860. He also owned a male slave, age twenty-six, which is how old her great-great-grandfather, John, would have been in 1860. Moreover—and this is very important—he owned a male slave, age five, which is how old Oprah's great-grandfather, Harry Lee, would've been in 1860! No other slaves in the county match these three ages and relationships of proximity to a white person named Lee.

Matching ages and genders of slaves listed in the 1850 or 1860 slave schedules with freed men and women listed in the 1870 census is not absolute proof of identity, but it is an important place to start. Accordingly, it is reasonable for us to conclude that these three people are quite probably Oprah's ancestors on this side of her family, her direct ancestors who were born into slavery and remained in slavery until the end of the Civil War. We were lucky in that this is the only slave owner named Lee in the state of Mississippi whose slaves' ages matched that of her ancestors. And we looked at every Lee in the entire state.

Oprah was deeply moved when I showed her S.E. Lee's slave schedule. This seemingly simple document, a document almost 150 years old, listing human beings as objects of property, bore the sole evidence of her ancestors' existence. She was, I believe, shocked to see just how stark it all was, how matter of fact, how, as it were, black and white: There were her forebears, written down as possessions, their ages and color recorded, but not their names. Oprah began to cry. And she cried, I think, because she was shocked to see two human beings from whom she is directly descended listed merely as nameless objects along with "the chickens and the cows," as she put it.

It's always distressing to see such tangible evidence of what we already know—that the entire system of slavery was an attempt to objectify our slave ancestors, to rob them of their humanity. But when one looks at a record of such objects of "property," and then realizes that this object here, and that object there were, in fact, one's great-great-grandparents, then research becomes a "whole nother" order of thing, a time-machine through which we can, at last, penetrate the veil of slavery, allowing the silenced ancestors to speak their own names! As painful as it is, this realization is also exhilarating. And I wish every African American could be able to experience it—in all of its pain and pleasure—just as Oprah Winfrey was able to. All of us are descended from men and women who were nothing more than property—listed along with the mule and the ox and the cow, the hoe and the plow. They were objects of commerce; slavery was a business.

"That's one of the reasons why I work so hard," said Oprah, after

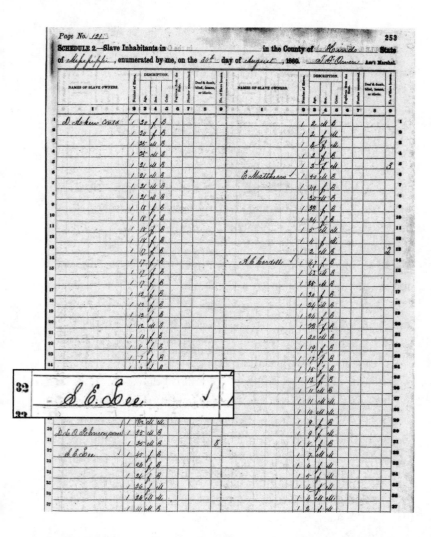

An 1860 Hinds County, Mississippi, Slave Schedule listing slave owner S. E. Lee on line thirty-two with fourteen slaves; most probably including John, age twenty-six; Grace, age twenty-six; and Harry, age five. John and Grace are Oprah Winfrey's maternal great-great-grandparents, and their son, Harry, is Oprah's great-grandfather, Harry Lee. *Public Domain*

a long silence. "And I feel like I have not even the right to be tired, ever, because I know I come from this. I didn't know names and backgrounds, but I know I come from this." Indeed, and so do we all.

As I mentioned earlier, it turns out that Oprah has been collecting slave documents for many years, in a systematic manner, almost like a scholar would. (In fact, perhaps the biggest surprise about Oprah Winfrey, for me, in the course of this whole project was learning about her love of black history; she may not quite be obsessed, but it's close!) Once when I visited her home in Montecedo, when she was filming her magnificent Legends Ball, she showed me a number of the artifacts she owns. She keeps them in her home, some framed and hanging on her walls, where she can regularly refer to them—as a kind of inspiration or motivation. I do the same thing, both in my office and at home, but I suppose that I'm expected to do this, as a professor of African and African American studies. The depth of Oprah's passion for African American history is quite impressive: "I see them regularly," she said. "Sometimes I'll just go and I'll look at their names and how they're listed, by only first names and ages and prices. And I'll think, This is all their lives meant to this person, and to a community, and a country."

I asked her whether her family ever talked about slavery when she was growing up. As most of us would respond truthfully, she said no, absolutely not. "When you grow up poor and on welfare," she continued, "you don't have time to think about what came before. You're just like, Can I get the light bill paid? And the insurance man's at the door, tell him I'm not home."

This is true, of course, but then I suggested that there might be another reason as well—a reason I've contemplated many times regarding the lives of all black Americans, be they rich, poor, or somewhere in between. For years and years, we were embarrassed about slavery. We were embarrassed about our slave past. That's

Still from *Beloved,* the 1998 film based on the book by Toni Morrison. In it, Oprah Winfrey plays Sethe, a freed slave haunted by the ghost of her dead child. © *Harpo, Inc. Photograph by Ken Regan.*

why I think it's so extraordinary that our generation is embracing our slave heritage.

Oprah agrees. "When I did the movie *Beloved,*" she said, "it was not as successful at the box office as any of us would have wanted it to be, and I was asked by so many press people: 'Why would you want to tell this story?' And I wanted to tell the story because I find such pride in the story. My strength comes from their strength. And when I look at these documents, for me personally, and I think for us as a people, I think we owe them a resurrection. I think that the price that they paid for us, the indignities that were suffered, I mean, every day was a trial."

Turning back to her family tree, I showed Oprah the oldest generation on her maternal line that we can find—her great-great-grandparents Henrietta and Pearce Winters, who were both slaves born in Mississippi. The 1870 census tells us that Pearce was born around 1849, and the 1880 census tells us that Pearce married Henrietta, who was born in Mississippi in 1855 (Henrietta's last name is not recorded). This census also tells us that by 1880, Pearce and Henrietta lived in Attala County, Mississippi, with their five children, including Oprah's great-grandmother Amanda Winters.

I explained to Oprah that we could not trace her maternal line back any farther than this with certainty. However, census records do give us some information that leads to some interesting suppositions. In 1870, Pearce was twenty-one and living near a man named Jesse Winters, age thirty-nine, born in Georgia. Jesse Winters *could* be Pearce's father. There is no way to know for sure—but this speculation is supported by the fact that Pearce named one of his sons Jesse, and Pearce's 1880 census enumeration lists the birthplace of his father as Georgia.

Now, for a moment here, let's examine the process by which we can begin to speculate about Pearce's possible relation to the man who quite possibly could have been his father.

Jesse Winters was born in Georgia in 1831. We know this from census records. And we believe he was a slave owned by Leonard Winters, who was born in South Carolina in 1782, and that Leonard Winters lived in Georgia before coming to Mississippi (his son Benjamin was born there in 1833). In 1850, the slave schedule lists Leonard as owning seventy slaves, including a ten-month-old male infant, the exact age Pearce Winters would have been in October 1850. By 1860, Leonard was dead, but his son Benjamin F. Winters

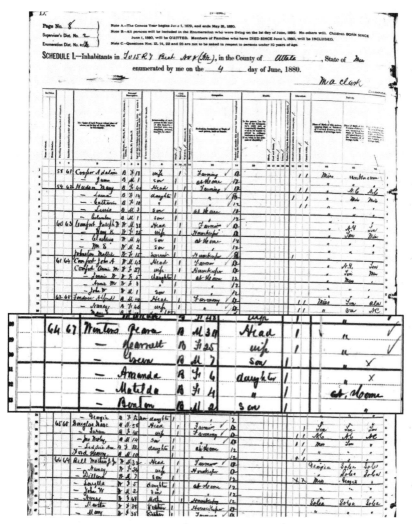

An 1880 Attala County, Mississippi, federal census showing Oprah Winfrey's maternal great-grandmother, Amanda Winters, as a six-year-old, living with her four siblings in the household of her parents, Pearce and Henrietta Winters. Amanda's father, Pearce Winters, is listed as a farmer, the occupation pursued by the vast majority of former slaves. *Public Domain*

owned a twenty-eight-year-old male who could be Jesse. Moreover, his widow owned sixteen slaves, including a ten-year-old male who could be Pearce. This is consistent with what historians know about the movement of slaves and their white owners through the antebellum South. Jesse Winters could have been part of a great forced migration of black slaves from the farmed-out areas of the eastern seaboard, including South Carolina and Georgia, to the frontier of Mississippi in the early 1830s, as the Native Americans who had lived there were ultimately forced out, making room for white settlers, settlers who often brought their slaves with them. In addition, as cotton production and farming increased in scale, large numbers of slaves were sold to businesses in Mississippi.

As you can see, when we get into the slave period, if we wish to learn anything at all about an individual slave, we have no choice but to study the records of the masters, and then to use the methods of historical detectives to piece together a "probably" tale. And I believe that in this case, it is reasonable to assume, because of all of these coincidences, that Jesse Winters most probably was Pearce Winters's father.

These details provided Oprah with a sense of who her ancestors may have been all the way back to 1830. Of course, let me be clear here: We don't know for sure that Jesse was related to Pearce. And we cannot go back any further. As of now, the Winters line ends with Pearce, and that's the farthest point back that we can take Oprah's maternal line. However, if we go back one more generation on Oprah's paternal line—her father's, Vernon's, line—we come to Sanford Winfrey's parents, her great-great-grandparents Constantine and Violet Winfrey. And here Oprah's deep roots grow even more fascinating. In fact, the story of Constantine Winfrey is the most remarkable story about a former slave in the Reconstruction Era that I have ever encountered. Its novelty, I believe, helps us to understand ever more fully why Oprah Gail Winfrey, well, came to be "Oprah."

Constantine Winfrey was born in October 1836 in Georgia. His wife, Violet, was born in North Carolina in 1839. She didn't have a last name—or if she did, it was never recorded. It seems that Violet was acquired in North Carolina, where she is listed as having been born, and shipped, somehow, to Mississippi. Constantine and Violet were married around 1859. They had eight children together.

Oprah knew that the Winfrey name came from this man, Constantine—she had heard of him in her family's lore and she knew him to be the highest branch on the family tree—but she never heard anything more about him. And she had no idea where his last name came from. I think we found out. Constantine Winfrey probably took his name because he was a slave owned by a man named Absalom F. Winfrey. In the 1870 census, Constantine is listed as living three houses down from Absalom and Absalom, like Constantine, had also moved to Mississippi from Georgia. Furthermore, an 1860 slave schedule indicates that Absalom owned seven slaves, the profile of one of whom fits Constantine exactly!

The 1880 census tells us that Constantine's mother was born in South Carolina; his father, in Georgia. Constantine may have come to Mississippi in 1850 with James H. Davidson, father-in-law to Absalom Winfrey. We can assume this if we compare the 1850 and 1860 slave schedules of the two men, a comparison that suggests that Constantine could have been willed to Absalom upon Davidson's death. In 1850, Davidson owned a male slave identified as thirteen years old; in 1860, Absalom Winfrey owned a male slave identified as twenty-three years old. In 1870, Constantine Winfrey

Absalom Winfrey (*in foreground*) with his wife, Sarah, and family. Absalom Winfrey is believed to be the slaveowner of Constantine and Violet Winfrey, Oprah's paternal great-great-grandparents. *From the personal collection of Bill Winfrey*

identified himself as thirty-five years old. Could this be the same person, or is this a coincidence?

There is no concrete proof that Constantine was owned by Absalom, or that he took his name, but such an assumption is reasonable. I am convinced that Constantine took his name from his old owner, given the unusual occurrence of that name in the surrounding region.

As for who Constantine was, we uncovered some quite remarkable things about him. The 1870 census lists Constantine and Violet as "Conston Tine and Vilot Tine," along with the five children living then. We know that these people are Constantine and Violet Winfrey because of the names of their children. "Conston Tine" was thirty-five at the time, "male, black; place of birth Georgia; farmer. Cannot read, cannot write." And Vilot Tine: "Cannot read, cannot write." This is of course to be expected, since almost all slaves were illiterate. But I learned something remarkable about Constantine, something that would prove to be consistent among later generations of Winfreys, including Oprah. I did so by comparing this census to the one that followed it ten years later, in 1880. That census lists Constantine and Violet again, but it indicates that Constantine can read. And he can write. In ten years, Constantine Winfrey learned to read and write!

Oprah and I were dumbfounded. Can you imagine what it meant for this man to read after it had been forbidden to African Americans under slavery for so many years? At thirty-five, as a newly freed slave, he couldn't read and he couldn't write. At forty-five, just ten years later, he could both read and write. In ten years, he had mastered literacy as an ex-slave. And that's mastering literacy while he's still having to work as a farmer every day, pick cotton, earn a living, raise and take care of a growing family. It's not as if he could afford to be a full-time student, enrolled in a school.

What's more, Oprah's great-great-grandfather not only embraced education himself but emphasized education to his children and to the rest of the colored section of his hometown. We located a report from the Montgomery County School Board dated 1906, which reads: "On petition it was ordered that Spring Hill Col[ored]

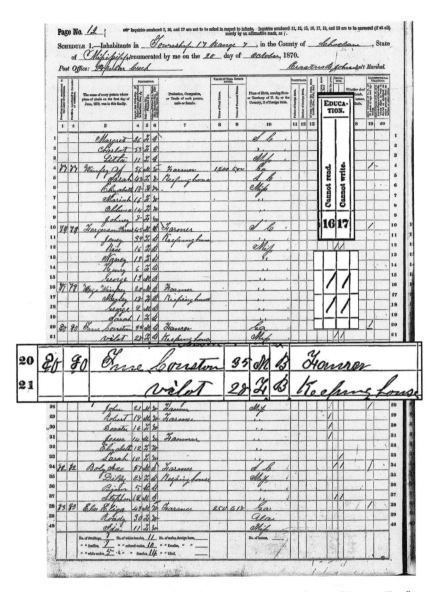

The 1870 Choctaw County, Mississippi, federal census showing "Conston Tine" and "Vilot Tine" (Constantine and Violet Winfrey), Oprah Winfrey's paternal great-great-grandparents. In this enumeration, neither Constantine nor Violet could read or write. *Public Domain*

The 1880 Montgomery County, Mississippi, federal census enumeration, in which Constantine Winfrey is shown as being able to read and write. By comparing Constantine Winfrey's 1870 enumeration to this document, we learned that Constantine taught himself to read and write in the decade after he obtained his freedom. *Public Domain* schoolhouse in Beat 5 be moved to a point on Consta[n]tine Winfrey's place."

Constantine Winfrey moved an entire schoolhouse so that the black children in his community could get an education! This action must be understood within its historical context. In Mississippi in the late 1800s, the rise and fall of Reconstruction—between 1866 and 1876—led to intensely exacerbated racial tensions. The Memphis massacre of 1866 took place 150 miles north of Poplar Creek, and the Clinton Massacre of 1875 took place just 100 miles south. We've also found a complaint to the local Freedmen's Bureau office by a former slave (a neighbor of Constantine's) who had been shot in the leg by his former master for supporting the Republican Party, the party of Lincoln—revealing the kind of tensions that were building in Poplar Creek. Education was the hope of the former slaves, and for that reason, the dominant threat to their former owners' desires to keep them in a subjugated position, "by any means necessary," as Malcolm X once put it, in another context. Constantine Winfrey obviously knew this, as passionate and as determined as he showed himself to be in so quickly mastering literacy. And he shared that passion by providing the land for the black community's school.

Why did people on both sides of Oprah's family care so deeply about literacy and education? We don't have a simple answer. Even Oprah didn't know. But she was affected strongly by the revelation. "I can't even begin to explain what that is," she said, "but I think it's deep that that is where I've come from. I mean I've always sort of understood on the periphery and also inside myself how important education is, but I didn't know that that was the root of where I came from."

Indeed, as we have seen over and over, through several of her ancestral lines, Oprah is at the tail end of a long line of people who loved education. While I cannot prove this scientifically, I happen to

Meeting of The County School Board of Ed.

The County School Board met pursuant to call Aug. 25th 1906 with the following members present. J. C. Applewhite of Beat 1, C. C. McCoy of Beat 2, J. L. Wray of Beat 3, H. H. Kyre of Beat 4, and H. J. Carticher of Beat 5, present.

On motion, the matters of Beat 5 were considered first.

On petition, it was ordered that Spring Hill Col. Sal. Church in Beat 5 be moved to a point on Constatine Winfreys place about 3/4 of mile north of its present site, and that without cost to the County, ...

... less 10 acres, ... less 3 acres, and N.W.¼ of S.W.¼ less 10 acres, Sec. 20, Township 17, Range 7 E.

Proceedings of Beat 4

Upon petition, it was ordered that Kyre Hill (col) school house be moved as prayed for. Viz: From its present location to near New Hope Church. (col) on Lindsey Bridge Public Road and with cost to the County.

Proceedings of Beat 3

Upon petition, it was ordered that Forest school house be moved from its present location to a more convenient place, Viz: To a place in the S.E. corner of Webb Woods place, on the Lodi Road, near the 4 mile board.

Proceedings of Beat 2

An official order written by the School Board of Montgomery County, Mississippi, in 1906. The crucial lines of this document read: "On petition it was ordered that Spring Hill Col[ored] schoolhouse in Beat 5 be moved to a point on Consta[n]tine Winfrey's place about 3/4 of mile north of its present site, and without cost to the County." From this, we first learned that Oprah's great-great-grandfather Constantine Winfrey moved an entire schoolhouse so that the black children in his community could get an education. *From the personal collection of Oprah Winfrey, © Harpo, Inc.*

believe that this is why she is who she is. Or rather, it is deeply reflective of who she is. But there is another side to the story of her roots—another element that has defined her family since Constantine. And that element is the ownership of land, a factor as crucial as education to the shaping of her family.

I wanted to discover how Constantine supported himself after slavery. Where did he get this land that he used to feed his family for generations, the land to which he moved this schoolhouse? That Constantine was able to save the black community's school by moving the school building to his own land demonstrates the complex importance of land ownership not only to an individual but also to our broader community. Constantine Winfrey's ownership of property was not just about making money or being financially independent; it also enabled him to support philanthropic activities, such as enabling education to continue to be offered to all the black children in his community, not merely his own.

But how in the world did he do it? How did an illiterate exslave in 1870 eventually come to own acres and acres of prime farmland within just a couple of decades?

To answer all these questions, I turned first to Johni Cerny, and then to Jane Ailes, genealogists extraordinaire. Johni Cerny searched through surviving land deeds in Mississippi and discovered where Constantine's land was, and how he obtained it. As it turns out, it was beautiful, fertile land, well situated with a stream flowing through the middle. Constantine purchased it in two different parcels. And the story of those purchases—contained in the land deeds and mortgage agreements—is the only story of its kind that many other historians of this period and I have ever encountered.

Constantine bought the first parcel in 1876 from a white man named John R. Watson. It was obtained through a highly unusual means of payment. According to the deed signed by Watson in

1876, Constantine agreed to give him eight bales of "lint" or cleaned cotton in exchange for eighty acres of land. But there was a catch: Constantine didn't have any cotton. To get his land, he had to grow it and pick it first. According to the deed, Watson gave Constantine usage rights on the eighty acres with the understanding that in two years, Constantine would produce his eight bales. Now according to their agreement, each bale of lint cotton had to weigh 400 pounds. So that's 3,200 pounds of cotton. And to get this much clean cotton—"lint cotton," as Watson's agreement with him prescribed—Constantine probably had to grow and harvest about twice as much because of all the debris and detritus that is contained in harvested cotton. In other words, this means that Constantine had to grow and pick and clean about 6,400 pounds of cotton, and do so in two years!

Now, remember: John Watson is a white man and this is 1876, the year Reconstruction ended. Needless to say, this was a very bad time for blacks. Moreover, throughout the 1870s, the entire country was in terrible economic shape. There was essentially a depression that lasted the whole decade. So white people were poor, and black people were poorer. Moreover, politically, it was a nightmare for black people because as Reconstruction was ending, the Old South was rising again, and many if not most of the gains that black people had made in the decade following the Civil War were about to be wiped out.

These are the circumstances under which Constantine signed this agreement, promising that he would harvest this monster load of cotton in just two years. In addition, the agreement stated that if he could not deliver the eight bales of cotton in the allotted time period, he was "toast," as we might say today. Actually, the deal was that in the first year, he was supposed to deliver four bales of cotton. If he couldn't do that, then he could provide two bales of cotton instead, but these bales had to weigh five hundred pounds each—not four hundred—as rent for the first year. This means that if he couldn't harvest enough cotton, then he'd have to pay rent the first year, and not his mortgage payment. If at the end of the second year he didn't deliver his eight bales of cotton, he would be forced to vacate the land. In effect, Constantine Winfrey signed a two-year mortgage, with full payment due at the end of the agreed-upon time. It was all or nothing by the end of the two years.

Constantine had a lot of chutzpah. And he had a lot of work to do to satisfy this commitment while feeding his family. But, some-how, he pulled it off. And we know that because we found two deeds, both recorded in 1881—a deed of conveyance and mort-gage (signed in 1876 by Watson), and a second deed of conveyance recorded in 1881 (signed in 1881 by Watson's heirs)—indicating that Constantine Winfrey had satisfied his obligation and owned his land free and clear. Of course, there is a mystery here. Why did five years elapse between the initial deal between Constantine and Wat-son in 1876 and the deed that finalizes it in 1881? Didn't the initial deal say that Constantine had only two years to grow the cotton? Shouldn't he have gotten his deed in 1878? What happened?

We don't know. But Jane Ailes found out that John Watson died in 1877, and then his widow and son honored his deal with Constantine. So perhaps there was some delay in completing the paperwork. In any case, the paperwork was largely a formality—that Constantine was still on the land in 1881 is evidence that he harvested, cleaned, and delivered his cotton within the required two-year window.

What's more, Jane Ailes also found a third deed from 1882 indi-cating that Constantine had purchased a second plot of land—another eighty acres adjacent to the Watson plot. He paid $250 for this plot in 1882, which was a lot of money and which indicates that he must have been doing very well in developing his first eighty acres.

The 1876 deed that indicates that Constantine Winfrey bought eighty acres of land from John Watson in exchange for eight bales of lint cotton. *Public Domain*

And, indeed, Ailes examined the 1880 census and found an agricultural schedule that listed the number of acres that Constantine owned, how he was using it, all the animals he owned, and the products that he produced.

According to this schedule, he had three milk cows and one other cow. One calf was born that year; and another cow was slaughtered. He produced three hundred pounds of butter in 1879 and he owned thirteen pigs and thirty-five barnyard chickens. He produced fifty dozen eggs. He also had fifteen acres planted in Indian corn, which yielded two hundred bushels of corn; three acres of oats, which equated thirty bushels; twenty acres of cotton, which yielded five bales; and four acres of cow peas. He also produced one hundred gallons of molasses from two acres planted in sorghum. Constantine Winfrey was a busy man, learning to read and write—no doubt at night—after all of this farmwork was done.

So Constantine managed to be a thrifty, productive farmer at a time when the status and power of black people were falling apart in the South. Constantine Winfrey, somehow, through sheer grit and energy and determination, managed to thrive. This is a remarkable story: A black man makes a deal with a white man eleven years after the end of the Civil War, in Mississippi, of all places, and the white man—rather, his widow—honors the deal. This black man now owns a very nice piece of land, mostly cleared bottomland, with a gentle, treed hillside and a stream running through it—and no one tries to take it away from him. What's more, on a deed of trust for a loan signed in 1883, Constantine signs his full signature. He's not signing with an *X,* as does his wife, Violet; he's literate and he can sign his own name. Remember: Just a little over a decade ago, he was illiterate.

Constantine Winfrey's land deed was unusual as well as extraordinarily rare. No historian with whom I have discussed this story has heard of a similar instance where a black man used cotton as the payment of a mortgage in the former slaveholding South. I think this man was a hero.

When we think of black history, we tend to think of heroes like Frederick Douglass or Booker T. Washington, Sojourner Truth or Harriet Tubman—people, in other words, who made grand contributions to our people. But this man showed a heroism that was just as authentic—and meaningful—a hero on the ground. Let's consider his achievement in its historical context: A black man, barely literate, walks up to a white man in 1876, the year that Reconstruction ends, a year in which the newly freed slaves are more vulnerable than they have been in a full decade, and makes a deal with that white man that he'll deliver approximately 3,200 pounds of hand-picked, cleaned cotton in return for eighty acres of land. The black man picks it, delivers the product, and the white man's widow honors his agreement! In all my years studying African American history, I had never heard of such an audacious act by a black man in the era of Reconstruction.

Precisely when the rights of most, if not all, black people in the South were being trampled upon by vigilante groups such as the Ku Klux Klan, Constantine Winfrey had the audacity to strike such a bargain—some would say, a bargain with the Devil—and believe that he could meet its terms (picking all that cotton, all the while farming to keep his family alive) and also trust the white man to keep his word. The white man could easily have cheated him. He had all the power over the transaction, including the capacity to nullify it. Constantine could have shown up dutifully with his eight bales of cleaned cotton, and John Watson could easily have said, "No, it's only seven bales," or, "I only agreed to give you ten acres, not eighty." Or anything! But none of that happened. The deal was honored.

For African Americans, buying land represented the first step in freeing themselves from the legacy of slavery and the subsequent servitude of sharecropping. It was generally difficult for blacks to purchase land—in practice, if not legally—during this time. A host of informal practices kept them from doing so, and would keep them from doing so, in proportion to their share of the population in the South, for generations to come. For example, banks or individuals wouldn't loan money to blacks, whites wouldn't sell to blacks who could afford to purchase the land or make the necessary mortgage payments, and so on.

I suspect most of us are familiar with the phrase "forty acres and a mule," if only because Spike Lee named his film company that. Near the end of the Civil War, Gen. William Tecumseh Sherman promised the ex-slaves forty acres of tillable land, land that would have been redistributed from the land owned by slaveholders, land on which the freed men and women had been enslaved. This would have been the most radical land redistribution program in the history of the United States. And it's the origin of that famous phrase. But that, we know, did not happen: Few ex-slaves got any land, let alone a mule. Yet Constantine Winfrey, somehow, did.

Oprah rightly sees this land for the heroic monument it surely is: This was the very first property that any member of her family ever owned. It was this farm that sustained and supported her family for generations. Just as important, it was this farm that played a crucial role in furthering the progress of the Poplar Creek, Mississippi, black community by becoming the literal foundation for their education. This is fascinating to an historian like myself because it's a patent reminder that the black community never consisted of one economic or social class. It had parts, or economic subdivisions. Even in the earliest years following slavery, the black community had a very distinct class structure, a structure that was sometimes based on color, sometimes based on education, sometimes based on property ownership, but all the time based on literacy. Among the slaves freed following the Civil War, this was really the start of the black middle class. (Of course, many blacks freed before the Civil War had become property owners before that war, sometimes even in the eighteenth century or before. And they, of course, constituted still another class within the African American community. Unfortunately, these Negroes freed before the Civil War sometimes exhibited a certain class prejudice against those blacks who weren't emancipated until after.)

These facts reveal that, at least since the nineteenth century, the African American community has been complex, with much social and economic variation. (Today, the class divisions have grown much bigger, especially with the onset of affirmative action diversity programs since the late 1960s. We have a much bigger middle class now than we've ever had.) What this means is that throughout African American history not everyone defined as "black" has experienced being black in precisely the same way. Whereas laws and their implementation no doubt could, and did, affect all black people in the same manner—I am referring to issues such as voting or riding on trains or marrying—the possession of literacy, the mastery of education, and the ownership of land all made for profound differences within the black community. They affected, sometimes determined, how freely a black person could live her or his life, even within the broader strictures of antiblack racism and Jim Crow segregation. Certainly, this was true of Oprah Winfrey's great-great-grandfather Constantine Winfrey, even in the state of Mississippi, which during the Civil Rights Movement was thought to be the most segregated state of all.

Stories such as those of John Watson striking a bargain to sell land to Constantine Winfrey are all too rare in our textbooks. If we encountered this story in a film, either Watson would abscond with the eight bales of cotton or the Klan would burn Constantine out shortly after he had constructed his new home. And, tragically, we know such betrayals did occur all too frequently. But such stories, no matter how rare, reveal how truly complex and variegated was the multilayered set of economic and social relationships between black people and white people in the postbellum southern United States. Stories such as these are no doubt far more common than previously imagined, and wait to be discovered in the historical records of our individual ancestors, hidden under the lush foliage of the branches of our family trees.

Genealogy, in other words, is history from the gene up, history from its most particular manifestation to its broader implications.

Unless more African Americans tell their family's story, the full range of the larger narrative of our people's experiences as Americans cannot even begin to be told.

Constantine Winfrey's remarkable story is where the paper trail of Oprah Gail Winfrey's family tree ends; put another way, the Oprah Winfrey family saga ends, or begins, with Constantine and his wife, who outlived slavery and made their respective marks on history. Prior to them, however, there's no written record of any of Oprah's ancestors, at least none that we've yet been able to find. And this barrier in the time line, at the beginning of the nineteenth century, is overwhelmingly common in tracing African American family history, despite the fact that almost *half* of the 500,000 or so slaves imported to the United States from Africa arrived in this country before 1760. The stories about Oprah's relatives have shown me how the former slaves made a way out of no way—how they persevered during the incredibly difficult transition from slavery to freedom. They laid the foundation upon which we've built our history and our culture. They are our roots, we are their branches, the roots and the branches of the great African American people.

But what of the men and women who came before there was a paper trail of their existence, all of the men and women of whom history has left us no written clue? What of them? What of all of those unfilled branches on the upper reaches of our family trees? Almost all that we've learned about our newly freed ancestors comes from public documents recorded after the Civil War. What about the millions who lived their entire lives in slavery, from birth to the grave? Is it possible for us to find out something—anything—about them, about the missing links between the beginnings of our American heritage, and the last one of our ancestors who lived on the African continent, the person responsible on our family tree for our origins in sub-Saharan Africa?

PART FIVE

Beyond the Middle Passage: DNA

I was especially pleased that we could trace Oprah's family tree back into slavery, back to the earliest decades of the 1800s, yet there was so much more left to uncover. What about the very first generation of African Americans in her family, the people born in Africa, thrown into slave ships against their will—could we find any of them? Slavery stole their ethnic identities. Almost every black American wonders where our ancestors came from in Africa. What languages did they speak? What was their music like? Their religion? Their culture? These are questions that generations of African Americans have asked and hungered to have answered, but most of us have presumed that the answers to these questions are long lost, buried under the waves of the Atlantic Ocean in the silences created by the dreaded Middle Passage.

Professional genealogists like Johni Cerny have repeatedly told me that it is virtually impossible to trace an African American family back to its first ancestor, the person who was somehow dragged onto a slave ship in Africa, to identify them by name and tribe. And Cerny is not some dire nay-saying pessimist. From her experience, she believes that every African American should be able to trace at least one ancestor back before 1870, and that as many as 10 or 15 percent of us will be able to trace an ancestor back to the eighteenth century. But none of us, she believes, will be able to get back to Africa through a paper trail.

Cerny herself has never been able to do it, and she's been doing black genealogies since 1977. Moreover, she doesn't know a single colleague who has ever managed to do it. As we have seen, the slave system made sure of that by eliminating our ancestors' names. And without names, you can't find adequate records through which to reconstruct your family's history. Of course, the slave ships kept very detailed records, including manifests that listed every piece of "human cargo" on board every ship. Except for records kept by the

Portuguese in Angola, however, the manifests contain only head counts of the slaves who were brought to America, not their names. And so there is no way to know what happened to those people once they stepped onto and off the boat. They went to an auction where they were sold, or to a master who had already paid for them. They had African names before they came here, but they were stripped of those names—as well as their language and their religion. It all went away. And with no names, you have no records, and with no records, you have no trail to trace.

Fortunately, we now have new clues about our past, thanks to recent developments in DNA science. When printed records run out, as they inevitably do, genetics can take over. Our ancestors brought something with them that not even the slave trade could take away—their own distinctive strands of DNA. And because their DNA has been passed down to us, their direct descendants, it can serve as a key to unlocking our African past.

There are a number of companies that can try to help you trace your family back to Africa by testing your DNA. There is a charge for these tests, ranging from about $100 to $300. I realize that will be a significant obstacle for many, but the process can cost less than an expensive pair of tennis shoes, and prove much more valuable in the long run. However, I strongly recommend that you don't rely on just one company's test, that you have yourself double tested, and that you do your own research into the history of Africa so that you can better understand and evaluate the results of your tests. I realize that that will add significantly to your costs and to the demands on your time, but I believe the results will be well worth it.

If you choose to make this journey, it begins with a simple and painless procedure: collecting cells from the insides of your cheeks. From these, geneticists extract small sections of our DNA. The acids within them, referred to by the letters *A, C, G,* and *T,* form distinctive sequences. Known as haplotypes, these sequences can then be compared to DNA samples taken from around the world. A match means that we've found someone with whom we share a common ancestor. And back in Africa, scientists have spent several decades asking tens of thousands of Africans to do the same thing. So a match between an American's DNA and an African's DNA could reveal an ethnic identity that has been lost for centuries.

To help Oprah take this step, I enlisted the help of a number of scientists who use genetic ancestry tracing in their research—Dr. Fatimah Jackson at the University of Maryland, Dr. Peter Forster at the University of Cambridge, Dr. Rick Kittles at Ohio State University, and Dr. Mark Shriver at Pennsylvania State University.

Dr. Kittles draws on his own original database of more than 25,000 African sequences. Meanwhile, Dr. Jackson and Dr. Forster sift through every DNA lineage ever published. Dr. Shriver is a population geneticist who works at the forefront of admixture mapping: testing our DNA for evidence of ancestors from different continents.

All of these scientists are cautious—and very careful about explaining to me what we can and cannot learn from DNA. "When you look at any cell in the body," says Dr. Kittles, "any human cell, we find that there are twenty-three pairs of chromosomes. And within those twenty-three pairs of chromosomes there are what we call markers. Now, some markers vary significantly between individuals, between communities, and between continental populations. So from those markers, we can tell where your ancestors may have come from."

I asked Kittles if these markers determine what people generally refer to as "race"—and I was pleasantly surprised by his answer.

"No, no," said Kittles, "that's not what we mean by race. Race is more a social concept than a biological entity. We talk about human biological races, but it's difficult to assess or to measure human race in a biological sense. We use these markers to assess variability within a family or a population or a community. We use them to infer ancestry—to estimate or predict who is related to who, who may have shared ancestry, which communities have shared ancestry, and the like."

I asked Kittles, jokingly, why, if race is more social than biological, do I have kinky hair and thick lips? He laughed and told me he was certain several of my ancestors had those features—just like his ancestors did. "But you can't isolate that in a test tube," he said. "We know that many of those physical features are genetically determined, but right now we don't know which genes are involved and how many and how they are inherited and all of that." He then told me that a lot of active research is occurring regarding the genetics of skin color, and that he is very involved in this research. But, thus far, he says, little is known.

I had thought, naively, that there would be black genes, Indian genes, Asian genes, European genes. But that's not the case. "There are genes," says Dr. Kittles, "that are markers that are associated with continental groups but they are not exclusive or specific to any of the broad phenotypes like African, Indians, or the Europeans."

Before we tested Oprah, I had some tests done on myself. To my enormous surprise, I was told that my admixture test revealed that I was 50 percent European and 50 percent African. In other words, that means that I'm half white! (Or, as the scientists say, "half European," because most of my white ancestry came from Northern Europe.) Now, my family's always presumed that we had one white ancestor on my father's side. But my DNA indicates I had more than one white ancestor—that half of my ancestors were white. The explanation could be as simple as the fact that each of my great-grandparents was 50 percent white. More likely, it means that a white European female ancestor of mine mated with an

African male sometime between 1619 and approximately 1740. We know these dates because the first African slaves came to this country in 1619 and we can identify my first known female ancestor— Sarah Days—as being born in approximately 1760. And it is Sarah Days whose mitochondrial DNA I share, through my mother, Pauline Augusta Coleman; her mother, Maguerite Elizabeth Howard; her mother, Lucy Ellen Clifford; her mother, Elizabeth Redmond; her mother, Lucy Redmond; and her mother, Sarah Days.

According to family legend, one of my great-grandfathers, Edward Gates, was the son of a white slave owner and his former slave. But I never imagined that all my great-grandparents had so much European ancestry. In fact, two additional tests—of my y-DNA and my mitochondrial DNA—also traced my ancestry to Europe to Ireland on my father's side, and—among other exact matches—to two Ashkenazi Jewish women in northern Europe on my mother's side! How in the world did this happen? Of course, we all know that many slave owners impregnated their African slaves. But to see that story written so clearly in my own DNA was quite a shock. I'll never see my family tree—or myself—in quite the same way again.

This is a fascinating issue, with paradoxical implications. On the one hand, DNA seems to be turning ideas of racial purity upside down. And that's just as well. Our culture is full of evidence of how those ideas have poisoned the relationship between so-called black people and so-called white people. It's shaped how we, even in the African American community, have viewed one another. It's so tragic how very many of us have internalized racism, and turned something as arbitrary, as superficial, as skin color, or hair texture, or the shape of our noses and the thickness of our lips, into such a source of pain and shame, in the same way that Miss Miller discriminated against Oprah because her skin was darker and her hair was kinkier than hers.

On the other hand, it's quite a shock for a man like myself—after spending decades studying the African American past—to wake up suddenly knowing I am "half white," whatever that means! I couldn't help but wonder what I was going to learn about Oprah through her DNA—and how she would respond to this knowledge. Science has given us new hope that we can trace our ancestors—but it can also prove confusing, even frightening, to some people.

I tried to explore these issues with Oprah before we conducted her DNA analysis. I asked her how she felt about Africa when she was growing up—was it somewhere to which she wanted to be connected? As a teenager, was she embarrassed about the images of Africans she saw on television and in films? Today, she is deeply connected to Africa, devoting large amounts of her time and resources to humanitarian causes there, but she freely admits that growing up, she was embarrassed by her African roots, just as many of us in our generation were. "I was ashamed," she responded, "if anybody asked, 'You from Africa?' in the school. I didn't want anybody to talk about it. And if it was ever discussed in any classroom I was in, it was always about the Pygmies and the, you know, primitive and barbaric behavior of Africans. And so if I was in a classroom with other kids—I remember like wanting to get over that period really quickly. The bare-breasted *National Geographic* pictures? I was embarrassed by all of it. I was one of those people who felt, 'I'm not African, I'm American.' They were primitive. Primitive and barbaric is the way I thought Africa was."

Oprah's honesty was quite refreshing. And her feelings were common among most African Americans until very recently. Even the proudest American Negro got his or her images of Africa from Hollywood and television, and what were those images? In a word: Tarzan. Blacks were invariably depicted as savages—people who didn't speak English, ran around in grass skirts, and ate missionaries for dinner. As an adolescent, I recoiled just as Oprah did. But like Oprah, when I started to study Africa in college and in graduate school, as I began to understand more, I began to feel a deep connection to the place and its people. Today, like most African Americans, Oprah now sees Africa as it really is—a vast continent, full of diverse cultures, ancient civilizations, and boundless beauty. After centuries of separation, we're eager to reconnect on many levels: spiritually, economically, and politically.

I asked Oprah what she most hoped DNA would answer about her African ancestry.

She told me that she had often been told she was a Zulu—a descendent of that great South African nation. They are almost legends, the Zulu people—warriors who fought so hard and so effectively against the British for so many years. She said, "When I'm in Africa, I always feel that I look Zulu. I feel connected to the Zulu tribe." Descendents of the Zulus are often quite proud of their heritage, and Oprah has talked about her possible Zulu connection more than once on her television program. She said to me, just before I sent her the test kit that would enable Dr. Rick Kittles to analyze her DNA, that it would be a great shock if it turned out she was not a Zulu. I hoped, for her sake, that the test results would verify her instincts.

I was determined to find out. I asked Oprah to send several DNA samples to our scientists. And we had all the results triple checked, by three different geneticists. So we're quite confident about our results.

The first test that we ran is called an admixture test. This test analyzes the ancestral information contained in all twenty-two pairs of a man or a woman's autosomal chromosomes. It works like this: Because these contain segments of DNA from all of your possible ancestors, all the way back thousands of years, it's possible to determine what percentage of your ancestry comes from each of the following four major historical population groups: Sub-Saharan African, European or white, Native American, and East Asian. This is the test that told me I was half white.

I asked Oprah, based on what she knew of her family history, what she expected the result to be. Did she think she'd have white ancestry? Without hesitating, she replied no, absolutely none. And she was firmly convinced of this—which is unusual. As Oprah knows, female slaves were frequently raped by their masters—and many African Americans who can trace their roots back to slavery find that they have white ancestors due to this. Nevertheless, Oprah was convinced that she did not. I was skeptical. The odds, I thought, were strongly against her. She looks mixed to me, with a white man lurking in her past somewhere!

I was wrong, and Oprah was right. Apparently, she has absolutely no white ancestry. (When I told her this, she quipped, "Well that's good.") This test result demonstrates that genetic heritage is a lot more complicated than the naked eye can detect, or than anecdotal or superficial observations can identify.

I also asked her about the possibility of her having Native American ancestry. She felt that this, too, was unlikely—but for different reasons. Quite perceptively, I think she understands that many African Americans have had fantasies about being descended from a Native American—as a way of escaping the social stigma of blackness in American society. She said to me that when she was growing up, every black child "wanted to have a little Indian blood—because you wanted to be anything other than colored." And this jibes with my own experience, growing up in the 1950s and 1960s.

I asked her why she thought this was so. "I was born at a time when to be anything other than colored was more admirable than to just be colored. So, the Native Americans, who were just as oppressed as we were and still are oppressed—it was still better to be them, or be like them, or have some part of them in you that said, 'I'm not completely colored, I'm not all Negro, I have something else.' And that was just ingrained. I remember standing out in my yard in Mississippi with people down the road and cousins and everybody talking about, 'Well, my grandmother, she Indian. Your grandmother not. My grandmother she is.' You know? We'd make up to be anything other than who we were."

This was a profound insight—one that strongly resonated with me. I, too, remembered that desire to be anything but black— and the willingness of folks to lie about it, if need be. The American Indian was always an extremely popular choice for our putative race-mixing in the distant American past. Oprah, too, had heard that one of her grandmothers was part Indian, but she said she really didn't believe it.

But Oprah's DNA told a different story. The admixture tests indicated that she was 89 percent Sub-Saharan African, 8 percent Native American, and 3 percent East Asian. The East Asian component can be explained by the fact that Native American ancestry often shows up in these tests as East Asian. Therefore, we can say that Oprah's Native American percentage is probably 11 percent. Accordingly, in Oprah's line, somebody, somewhere did, indeed, intermingle with Native Americans, most probably after the 1820s in Mississippi, when the first white settlers brought their slaves with them to settle from the Upper South, in lands left by the displaced Indians. Also, her Native American ancestry could come from the Carolinas or Georgia, where some of her ancestors lived before being moved to Mississippi. This would not be the first time that the genealogical evidence of Oprah's family's past would be useful in interpreting the genetic results, as we shall see.

Again, Oprah was pleased with the results. She said she was surprised but thrilled. "I feel more connected to where I've come from," she said. "And you know, I've never not appreciated Native Americans, but I will look at that culture differently now. I'll say brother and sister in a different way. And it's all so fascinating, the whole makeup of human beings and how we've all migrated." But, of course, what Oprah really wanted to hear about were her African roots. And another DNA test began to tell us something about them. Unlike the admixture test, this test focuses on sections of our DNA that we inherit unchanged from our female ancestors—our mitochondrial DNA. By analyzing Oprah's mitochondrial DNA, it's possible to learn about her matrilineal line—her mother's mother's mother's line—back through time. Remember that our genealogical research had only been able to take Oprah's matrilineal line back to Henrietta Winters, born in Mississippi around 1850. Henrietta was as far as we could go. That's where her matrilineal paper trail ended. But Oprah's DNA would allow us to go back to Henrietta's mother, and her mother, and on and on, all the way back to Africa. This is quite marvelous, if you pause to think about it, something of a miracle in the history of the diaspora of black Africans to the New World.

Dr. Fatimah Jackson explained the mitochondrial test. She told me that by comparing a specific segment of anyone's mitochondrial DNA with a number of sophisticated databases of DNA samples taken from African people living across the Continent today, we can find where a person's matrilineal ancestor comes from, even if that person was taken into slavery and brought to the New World in the hold of a slave ship. "It doesn't give you all of your maternal ancestors," Jackson said, "but it does give you the oldest female. Basically we're working on the premise that we start off with a small population in Africa in our collective motherland. The groups are small. They're clan units or even smaller tribal units, and as they move, they encounter new environments but most of the mating is within the group. So you tend to get concentrations of certain genes within those small populations within a relatively short period of time. As the groups move across geographical space, they are fairly isolated, not completely isolated of course, but somewhat isolated. And a mutation may appear. And that mutation then will spread throughout the group over a period of generations. And so we can track the mutation history of mitochondrial DNA, and that pretty much follows the population movements of females."

Using this test, we found identical mitochondrial DNA matches between Oprah and members of ethnic groups, or "tribes," in three parts of Africa—the Kpelle people in Liberia, the Bamileke people in Cameroon, and a Bantu-speaking people in Zambia. We also found identical matches to her DNA among the Gullah people off the coast of South Carolina and Georgia.

These various results made me nervous. On the one hand, I was glad that we had in fact succeeded in securing exact matches for Oprah's maternal DNA. But on the other hand, unfortunately for Oprah, the results meant she could not be Zulu. Indeed, as it turns out, virtually none of the Africans brought to America as slaves had Zulu origins. The Zulu homeland in southeast Africa was simply too far away from the main centers of the trade for any Zulu person to have been captured and sold into the trans-Atlantic slave trade. Would Oprah be angry at me, or at Dr. Kittles, who was nowhere close to share her wrath? The thought crossed my mind to simply tell her she was Zulu and be done with the whole matter! But, of course, I couldn't do that.

"If you tell me that I am not Zulu," she said just before I had to tell her that she was not descended from a Zulu female, "I am going to be very upset." Well, here goes, I thought. Oprah needed a moment to process this information. She still feels that, spiritually, she is fundamentally related to the Zulu people—which is a very healthy way to think about our putative African or European ancestry. Similarly, I feel that I am spiritually connected to the Yoruba people in western Nigeria. I am connected somewhat to the Yoruba people intellectually as well, since I studied their culture in graduate school, under the direction of the Yoruba writer Nobel laureate Wole Soyinka, who gave both of my daughters Yoruba names. I love Yoruba culture, especially Yoruba music and mythology. But I have absolutely nothing to do genetically with the Yoruba people. Likewise, Oprah Winfrey has nothing to do with the Zulu people genetically. But she feels connected to the Zulu, and she is entitled to do so.

Despite not being of Zulu descent, Oprah nonetheless has a very rich African genetic heritage. As I have indicated, our tests revealed identical mitochondrial DNA matches in three parts of Africa—the Kpelle people in Liberia, the Bamileke people in Cameroon, and a Bantu-speaking tribe in Zambia. Zambia, Cameroon, Liberia—Oprah's genes seem to be spread all over the continent! And the identical matches to hers that we found among the Gullah people in South Carolina would turn out to be an important piece of evidence in identifying her maternal ancestor's African ethnic origins. The Gullah people are a unique African American community, which has preserved a large part of its African heritage.

Of course, I now had a new problem. We had found African matches for Oprah, but these matches took us right across the continent, from west Africa to central Africa. Such results pose an obvious dilemma, a dilemma that many of you could one day face if you pursue this testing. Somewhere in Oprah's family past is her first enslaved matrilineal ancestor—and there's only one first. How do we find out where that person came from, if the DNA test yields more than one "exact" result? The only way is to reason one's way through multiple results by contextualizing genetic research with historical research. Just looking at the genetics in isolation, in many cases, including this case, will not be sufficient to solve this puzzle. To be understood, the DNA results must be put in their historical, cultural, and geographical contexts.

Accordingly, I consulted with Professors John Thornton and Linda Heywood, a husband-wife team of historians who teach at Boston University who are among the most widely respected scholars of African history, Brazilian history, and the African slave trade on both sides of the Atlantic. They explained to me that Oprah's DNA shows up in so many different places because of the history of Africa—over centuries, even millennia, tribes migrated across the Continent, people were taken away as captives in wars, people simply didn't stay in the same region for generation after generation. African people, in other words, moved around just like every other member of the human community did.

More specifically, Thornton and Heywood believe that Oprah's links to Zambia indicate that some of her maternal ancestors were almost certainly part of the Bantu migration, which is one of the largest migrations in the history of the human community. A small group of Bantu-speaking Africans migrated out of a core area in what we think is southern Cameroon and basically peopled a huge percentage of the rest of central and southern Africa. This migration took thousands of years—from perhaps 2000 B.C. to 500 B.C.—and brought a totally new kind of genetic mixture to the central and southern African populations. Thus, Oprah's Zambian DNA result could possibly be explained by the Bantu migration. That was one theory, and a most plausible one.

While a Bantu-speaking ancestor from Zambia could not be ruled out, nor could a Bamileke ancestor who lived in the interior of modern Cameroon, Thornton and Heywood believe that Oprah's other exact matches—her DNA hits in Liberia and also among the Gullah people off the coast of South Carolina—combine ultimately to point toward a West African origin of her first enslaved matrilineal ancestor. Moreover, these results square nicely with the history of the slave trade.

Specifically, between 1801 and 1810, approximately 41,000

slaves came into the United States through the port of Charleston, South Carolina. Those slaves came from the following regions: almost half, 45.9 percent, according to the historian David Eltis, came from Angola; while about 7.8 percent came from the region of West Africa that we call Senegambia (Senegal, Gambia, Guinea-Bissau, and Guinea); 19.6 percent came from Sierra Leone and western Liberia; 5.2 percent from the Windward Coast (Ivory Coast and eastern Liberia); 11.6 percent from the Gold Coast, or present-day Ghana; 1.6 percent from Dahomey, present-day Benin; 7.0 percent from the Bight of Biafra, in eastern Nigeria; and 1.4 percent from Mozambique. Agents and principles from these regions acted as middlemen in a complex economy that involved many small kingdoms, or ministates, along with larger states, such as Futa Jallon Kingdom.

The country that we know as Liberia today, along the west African coast, is the home of the Kpelle people. Knowing that one of Oprah's exact matches was with the Kpelle, I consulted David Eltis's Trans-Atlantic Slave Trade database to see if I might learn more about how that ancestor might have arrived in the United States. The Trans-Atlantic Slave Trade database is a compilation of the records kept by shipping companies involved in the slave trade, and it is a remarkable tool for historians. It shows the port of origin for virtually every ship that brought Africans to America. From it, I learned that 19.6 percent of the slaves imported through Charleston were taken from the Sierra Leone and western Liberia region. And based on the various possibilities afforded by comparing the Trans-Atlantic Slave Trade database percentages of slaves imported from Africa during the first decade of the 1800s through Charleston with the results of Oprah's DNA test, I became even more convinced that the most likely possibility is that Oprah's female ancestor who was first captured into slavery and brought to the New World was a person we would identify as belonging to the Kpelle tribe today. That conclusion is bolstered by her exact match with a person who is descended from the Gullah people, who live on the Sea Islands, just off the coast of Georgia and South Carolina, since the slaves arriving into this country through Charleston could just as easily have ended up there.

Gullah (also called Geeche) refers to both the language spoken among the African descendants of the Carolina and Georgia Low Country as well as the people themselves. Thornton and Heywood were able to tell me a great deal about these people. "Before the 1930s," said Heywood, "scholarly references to the Gullah, written largely by white Americans, argued that it was a corrupt form of early English, and that very little African linguistic elements were evident. This biased view has now been replaced by linguistic and historical studies that show definitively that Gullah is a Creole language with significant borrowings from west and central African languages."

"During the eighteenth century," said Thornton, "the Carolina and Georgia coastal region and off-shore islands where Gullah language and culture emerged were isolated from the white mainland regions. The people were mainly enslaved Africans from the Upper Guinea coast—which is the region from Senegal to Liberia—and from Angola. They were mostly first-generation slaves involved in rice and indigo cultivation. Largely sheltered from direct contact with whites who preferred to live away from the pestilential coast, the population was free to develop their culture and language. Some of the major cultural contributions of the Gullah were the familiar Uncle Remus stories that author Joel Chandler made famous. Margaret Washington Creel, author of *A Peculiar People: Slave Religion and Community Culture Among the Gullahs,* suggested that the development of the African American church on the islands derived from the Poro society of Sierra Leone and Liberia."

I asked Thornton and Heywood to tell me about how the Kpelle came to America. How did a black person from a village on the coast of West Africa end up a slave in the Old South?

Thornton didn't hesitate to answer. "It is a likely possibility," he said, "that her ancestress was captured as a result of the many wars. There was a Muslim state in Futa Jallon, in present-day Guinea, in the 1750s and '60s, and they conducted wars every year to convert people to Islam. But they also captured people and they enslaved many people and they exported them. There were also wars within that area, and there was banditry within that area as well."

According to Thornton, one of the ways we can get a sense of the Kpelle is to study the writings of a German missionary by the name of Georg Oldendorp, who worked among the slaves and slave traders in the Danish West Indies in the eighteenth century. Oldendorp was a kind of protolinguist. "He actually questioned captive slaves," said Thornton, "because he wanted to find out about their religious background. So he asked people to tell him their stories about where they came from, what they did in those places, and also how they were enslaved. And he had five people that he talked to who identified themselves as being from the area where the Kpelle lived. And of these people that he interviewed, four of them were captured in wars in that area."

Heywood offers an alternative possibility: "If you look at enslavement histories, some of the English slave traders talked a lot about how people were enslaved because of marital disputes—adultery or people got pawned in exchange for a bride price, that kind of thing. This was not quite as common as warfare but it was right up there."

So some way or another, according to these two, Oprah's first enslaved female ancestor was a Kpelle who was probably captured, sold, and then transported by a caravan from the Futa Jallon highlands to the coast.

I asked Thornton and Heywood to tell me a bit more about the Kpelle people, who today number about half a million in Liberia and Guinea Conakry, Africa. Thornton told me that they speak a southern Mande language similar to the Susu- and Mende-speaking peoples who live in Sierra Leone and Liberia—and he gave me a good deal of information on their history. According to Thornton, in the sixteenth century, the Kpelle were integrated into the African Kingdom of Kwoya, which a seventeenth-century tradition says was founded by migrants from Mali led by a prince. "Before their conquest by the Liberian State at the end of the nineteenth century," he said, "the Kpelle lived in a series of small fortified towns located northeast of Monrovia, Liberia's capital. The region had been in contact with Europeans since the sixteenth century, often trading commodities like cloth and iron as well as a small number of slaves from the very beginning of this contact. The Kingdom of Kwoya lost its unity at some point in the seventeenth century—and this collapse may have been responsible for the rise of the several independent towns that slave merchants described in the eighteenth century."

Regarding the structure of Kpelle society, Heywood said, "The major institutions linking the independent Kpelle towns were the Poro and Sande Societies. These were ancient institutions, appearing in Portuguese accounts from the 1490s. The Poro was a men's organization—a part of Kpelle and many other societies in the region—and it was an initiation society based on ranked membership. And paralleling the Poro was the Sande Society, which functioned in much the same way as the Poro, but whose members were limited to women. During the period of the slave trade, visitors to the Liberian coast described how the Poro and Sande societies functioned. Both societies recruited their members across political boundaries, and the function of these organizations was political, in that they settled disputes between towns and between individuals. The organizations also played a major role in the religious and commercial life of the Kpelle."

Heywood then began to explain more definitively how a Kpelle might have ended up a slave in nineteenth-century Mississippi: "What we know is that in the territories of Georgia, Alabama, Mississippi—as they're opening up in the 1810s, 1820s, 1830s—if her ancestor starts from South Carolina, there was a land migration. We know that there was internal slave trading from the upper South to the lower South—the upper South being Virginia, North Carolina, South Carolina, and the lower South at this point would be Georgia, Alabama, Mississippi. And we know that planters, sometimes younger sons, would move off with slaves that may have had some expertise, or that they trusted, or that they just wanted for the frontier—to establish some new plantation in these new areas that are opening up."

Thornton and Heywood then wanted to know more about the person who may have owned Oprah's first matrilineal ancestor in America. I told them that based on census records and slave schedules that we'd found in Salt Lake City, we believe that Henrietta Winters was owned by John or Leonard Winters, two brothers from the Pendleton district in South Carolina.

Hearing this, Thornton became very excited. "Pendleton district is in the western part of South Carolina and this is an area that was just like Attala County in Mississippi a little bit later," he said. "And there was a treaty a few years before with the Indians, and now they were moving people in, and a lot of people descended on that territory in the late eighteenth and early nineteenth century. So now we definitely start looking toward Charleston as the place of import for her African ancestors. From about the 1780s onward, Charleston was the major importing center not just for South Carolina, but also for a whole trade going down into the Gulf. If the slaves came up to Mississippi from the south, a lot of times they ultimately came first to Charleston."

I found this all very compelling evidence. And it meshes perfectly with my own understanding of the subject. The fact that Oprah's DNA has been found among the Gullah people suggests that her first matrilineal ancestor came to the United States through South Carolina and that her owner later moved down the Mississippi—leading eventually to the birth of Oprah's oldest female ancestor, Henrietta Winters, born in Mississippi around 1850. From South Carolina, we can trace a path back across the Atlantic to the region of Africa now called Liberia.

Before the slave trade was abolished in 1808, half a million Africans were brought to this country as slaves, again according to Professor Eltis's invaluable Trans-Atlantic Slave Trade database. That means that, of the twelve and a half million Africans taken across the Atlantic in slavery, only 500,000 Africans were brought to the United States (the remainder went to the Caribbean and Latin America). For most black Americans—about 90 percent—these 500,000 Africans are our ancestral pool. They are the core source of what are now more than 35,000,000 African American citizens. And thanks to the shipping records left by the European slave traders, we know through which ports in which African countries these slaves were shipped. In conjunction with the DNA test results, these records are a priceless tool in tracing an African American's ancestry back to Africa between 1619 and the end of the Civil War.

We don't know who owned Oprah's first enslaved matrilineal ancestor in America, nor do we know this ancestor's name. But taking the genetic evidence and this historical evidence together, I think that it is overwhelmingly likely that Oprah was descended from the Kpelle people in Liberia and that her ancestor most likely was either captured in a battle or became a slave as a result of a marital dispute, as Thornton and Heywood suggest. Thus, I felt very confident telling Oprah that she shares ancestry with the 300,000 Kpelle people who still live in the rainforests of central Liberia.

Oprah was stunned by the news. "That's me," she said somewhat wistfully, looking at the charts of her DNA that I had handed her. "I'm Kpelle. I feel empowered by this." And no doubt the Kpelle will welcome Oprah as a long-lost sister, just as warmly as the Zulu have done.

When I met Oprah, I met a person who had lived for the past two decades as one of the most famous people on earth but who was unable to name her great-great-grandmother, much less the identity of her maternal ancestor's original African tribe. By the time we said good-bye, all that had changed. Of course, as I explained to her, we identified, through genetics, only one line out of the thousands of ancestors that she has—it's only her mother's mother's mother's line that mitochondrial DNA can trace. Our ability to travel back into the past is still in its infancy. As DNA databases grow and as genealogical research techniques develop, we'll be able to find, ever more exactly, the identity of more of our ancestors and excavate ever more deeply the roots of our family trees.

As we increase our ability to do this, we'll not only begin to heal the rupture and the wounds of the Middle Passage, but we'll also be able to stake our claim, ever more deeply, on the American tradition.

PART SIX

Looking Back

*I*t has been almost a year since I first interviewed Oprah and began this journey into her past. The experience has for me proved richly rewarding, just as I hope it has been for Oprah. The individual stories drawn from Oprah's family have made me reconsider many of the larger forces—social, political, racial, and religious—that have shaped the black experience in this country since our ancestors' arrival in the United States as slaves. These are things I've thought about my entire career as a scholar. Nevertheless, undertaking this project forced me to see these matters differently. Among other things, I learned that the relationship between white and black was far more complex on certain levels than standard history books would allow.

Almost every black family has a slavery story, a migration story, a Jim Crow story. The Winfrey family is a remarkable example of how many African Americans built productive lives for themselves, out of the ashes of slavery, starting with virtually nothing but determination and drive, and an almost irrational embrace of hope.

Now, there are many motifs that run through Oprah's story— some are troubling and tragic—such as motifs of exploitation and abuse in her own life and in the lives of her ancestors. But there are also two other recurring motifs, which seem to repeat throughout each of her generations: that of education—of prizing education as an end in itself—and that of the value of land. Education and property ownership: These are the two most important aspects of Oprah's family history, themes that we encountered again and again. She is a property owner's daughter and she is a property owner's great-great-granddaughter. And I think that's a remarkable legacy from a couple who, in 1860, were slaves who could neither read nor write. Five generations of black entrepreneurs begat one of the world's great entrepreneurs: Oprah Winfrey is the fifth-generation entrepreneur in her family.

There's a quote that I like a great deal that Oprah used once on her television show when a fifteen-year-old guest was very mouthy. Frustrated, Oprah said to her, "Do you know how many black people bled and died so that you could be where you are today? The crown has been bought. All you need to do is pick it up and put it on your head." It's a quote that was passed on to her by Toni Morrison, who heard it from James Baldwin, so it has a regal lineage. I was quite struck when I first heard her say it.

I asked Oprah, now that she knew so much about African American history from her family's involvement in it, if she thought that our people, especially this generation, had changed over time. "You know," she said, "at this time in my life I feel a sense of sadness for the generation after me because I think that we, our generation, did not pass this knowledge on to them in a way that was tangible, in a way so that they could feel it inside and out. So that they could understand that the reason why you have the life that you lead now is because the crown was already paid for. You didn't pay for the crown. You might pay for your bling now and you got all that stuff. But you didn't pay for the crown. And I think that somehow we've lost that."

I couldn't agree more. I fear sometimes that we've become two people, two communities within the African American community. And the values that even the poorest part of our community— Oprah's ancestors, my ancestors, and your ancestors—embraced, have been lost for a huge segment of our people. That's a topic for another book. Too often, we don't like to hear this said in public, or even to discuss it among ourselves. But it's the unpleasant truth. And that saddens me, in large part because too many of us have internalized our own oppression, discarding traditional black values of education, sacrifice, hard work, and deferred gratification, the very values that have led to the progress of our people since slavery, and which recent black immigrants from Africa and the Caribbean have embraced to achieve middle-class status in one generation or two. Incredibly, two years ago, over 50 percent of all black undergraduates at Harvard were first- or second-generation West Indians and Africans. I find that statistic astonishing.

We need to tackle these issues head on, especially addressing the forms of black behavior that perpetuate our people's cycle of poverty. We need to talk about school reform—about after-school programs that teach algebra, chess, computer skills, African and American history, and entrepreneurial skills. We need to analyze what it would take for the bell curve of class in the black community to conform to the bell curve of class in the white community. We need a new Civil Rights Movement—one based on individual accountability and individual responsibility, one that insists that the black community turn inward and take stock of itself, rather than merely blaming slavery, segregation, and white racism as the cause of all our ills.

We have a lot of work to do. But I have to say that Oprah Winfrey's family history is an incredible model for us all—the model of a family that truly did overcome tremendous obstacles, drawing on traditional black values, values that, ultimately, are the best American values, values rooted deeply in her family tree. And this is the principal social value of African American ancestry tracing, as far as I am concerned. Tracing one's family tree won't solve all of the problems facing Black America, but this sort of knowledge about one's past most certainly can help to ground our people in the very best that the African American tradition has achieved, the fundamental principles that enabled our people not only to endure, but to rise and thrive.

"I feel that all the time," said Oprah. "I know that is the truth of my past and that this heritage has brought me to where I am today.

And I feel like I gotta carry that on. I feel that there were such sacrifices made. I feel deeply, and have always, even when I could not explain it, a deep, deep connection to those who've come before me. I feel that for Grace and Elmore and all the names. I feel it for the ones that made the history book, and for the millions that did not. For all the people who marched, but for those who couldn't march. They were just out there washing clothes and ironing and taking them to the white folks' house, and cooking, and doing the best they could."

In the end, I think this is why I conceived this book and my PBS series—why I am fascinated with the construction of black family trees—because it represents a different way of telling African American history. Few historians can take the time to tell this story through all of these anonymous people, people scrubbing white people's kitchen floors and doing their laundry. This is a different way to discuss the richness of the African American past, from the ground up, from the kitchen to the board room, as it were. And I think more and more that the broader narrative of the African American people can only be told as we resurrect these particular, little stories, stories that only emerge when one decides to reconstruct their own family tree.

If you would ask an historian, "How important is it that this one black sharecropper traded cotton for land?" they'd say, "Statistically, it's not important, and in fact, it goes against the larger trend." But experiences such as Constantine's actually happened, and must become a part of the narrative of African American history. These little stories, which are huge stories for us individually and for our families, collectively make up the narrative of our people. This is how we got over slavery and segregation, lynchings and poll taxes. This is how we survived. This is how we overcame tremendously difficult odds to emerge as a people.

We can never forget that there are many large trends in black history, but normal, regular black people lived their lives, too, each and every day. They loved and hated, worshipped and sinned, worried and aspired. They were defeated, yet they triumphed. Together, they created a culture, one of the world's great cultures; they made a world, one with its own language, its own sacred and profane institutions, its own art and music and literature and dancing, its own ways of walking and thinking, shucking and jiving, dissipating and aspiring. They met the daily struggles of everyday life—the ordinary struggles that all human beings face—and I think many of the history books miss that. Hopefully, this book captured some of those struggles and triumphs—and hopefully it allowed you to see African American history differently. And maybe it will inspire you to trace your own family tree in the same way that Oprah Winfrey did.

I keep my family tree framed on a wall in my kitchen. I glance at it at least once every day. It gives me a sense of satisfaction that is difficult to explain. But it does: Just being able to read the names of several of my third and fourth great-grandmothers and grandfathers places me in the world just as surely, in its way, as does my birth certificate. At least, it feels that way to me. There is a certain comfort that arises from knowing the names of one's immediate ancestors. This is very reassuring for me.

This past Christmas, I gave my daughters copies of our family tree. The truth is, their eyes glazed over when they unwrapped their gifts. I received a predictable "Gee, thanks, Daddy. . . . What else did you get for us?" But I didn't mind so much; they'll never have to worry about the things that I found myself worrying about following my grandfather's funeral when I was ten, things like who my grandfather's grandfather was. The truth is that my daughters probably don't even care! They can take these things for granted.

But perhaps their children will care, or their children's children. However, I don't really care if they care or not. The record of our family's past is hanging on the wall of our kitchen for them to see if ever they want to; their family lineage has been established for all time. This is who we are as a family, who our people were, and are, and where they came from. And nobody in our family, ever again, has to wonder about their origins. That is the power of genealogy. And that, for an African American, is a marvelous thing.

APPENDIX

Resources for Building Your Family Tree

When I finished my first draft of this book, I gave it to a good friend of mine, looking for feedback. He wrote me a long, thoughtful note, primarily mingling praise with constructive criticism—all very helpful. But in his last few paragraphs, he seemed to drift into a kind of despair when he thought about searching for his own ancestors. The process I'd gone through with Oprah was, he felt, quite intimidating. He said he was trying to imagine himself setting out on a similar quest and, well, he couldn't imagine it. It was just way too daunting. "How long is it going to take?" he wanted to know. "Am I going to have to quit my job to go running around the country tracking down every old newspaper clipping and dusty land deed in every state where my ancestors lived?"

In the interest of placating my friend, and anyone else who may be similarly intimidated, let me say that there's no quick and easy way to build your family tree, but that doesn't mean you have to mortgage your home and take a two-year unpaid vacation to get it done. You can spend as much or as little time on your tree as you want—you'll start learning stuff right away, so there's a reward for even the tiniest bit of effort. And, of course, the more time you put into the process, the more you'll get out of it. As my professional genealogy guru Jane Ailes says, the deeper you go into researching each person on your tree, the more you'll come to feel like you know those people, the more interested you'll be in the work, and the less your tree will seem like just a list of names. That doesn't mean it's going to be easy, but it does mean that you can control the process a bit.

Furthermore, while there is also no one right way to build your tree, in my experience, there is a step-by-step methodology that you can follow which will help streamline the work. I described this methodology in detail in the pages you just read, but here it is in brief:

First, begin by gathering basic information regarding who your ancestors were, when they were born and died, and where they lived—all with the goal of starting to map out your family tree. Over time, you'll find out details about these people's lives that ultimately make the genealogical quest more interesting and fulfilling, but at the outset, focus on information and gather as much as possible. Write down everything you know about yourself and your family, then start interviewing your relatives. Talk to as many of them as you can stand to talk to. Meet with the oldest ones first—as they presumably have the least time left and can give you the most information on past generations. Ask them everything— their birthdays, anniversaries, where they lived and worked, who their siblings were, their parents, their colleagues and friends. (You never know what you may glean from a call to your long-dead grandmother's old best friend.) Bring a tape recorder and record the interviews, but also take good notes—write down everything that comes into your head, because you'll often think of things during an interview that won't be captured on the tape and you might want to ask questions about those things later.

Plan to do at least one follow-up interview with everybody you talk to. This is very important. Your grandfather's memory may change from the first interview to the second, or your uncle may remember something that you can take back to your grandfather for clarification, or God knows what. Just do multiple interviews. Also, when you conduct your interviews, ask your relatives if they have documents to support their memories—birth certificates, marriage licenses, diaries, newspaper clippings, anything, really. Take whatever they'll give you and make copies.

As you're conducting your interviews, you should be sorting out the data you're collecting. I'd suggest organizing it all into genealogy charts that trace bloodlines and grouping people in family units. You can post index cards on a wall, if you like, one with each family member's name on it, as well as their relevant dates and locations. Then you can make connections between individuals by using pieces of string or tape. I find that having a visual image of the family tree is a great organizational help—you understand the data better if you can see it in this familiar form.

At the same time, you need to start checking everything you've learned against the public record. Remember, don't just take what your relatives say as gospel truth, no matter how sweet and trustworthy they may seem. Go find some records to back it up. I'd suggest you start with census records. If you know the name of one of your ancestors, you can search for him or her in the census, which will allow you to place that person within a generation in a particular state, town, and county. From there, you can begin to flesh out their lives and relations by tapping into all possible record sources in that area. There's a lot you can do here. You can search marriage records, death records, cemetery records, Social Security applications, military records, immigration records, trial records, tax filings, voting records, land deeds, slave-trade records, wills and other estate records, newspaper obituaries, school records, funeral home records, and church records, as well as local genealogies, county histories, and private journals and letters. Wow. Reading that makes me dizzy. But don't let it overwhelm you. Just go slowly, generation by generation. Don't try to leap all the way back to the 1800s, or else you'll likely as not reach a dead end—or worse, waste your time researching somebody who isn't even related to you. If you go slowly, though, you'll build a solid tree and you'll find the records are much easier to work with.

Where should you look for these records? Professional genealogists often start by using a website called Ancestry.com. They log on, search by name to get an overview of what records are available on a given individual, and then they go to the libraries, archives, and historical societies to see the original records. For a lot of research—including census research—my professional friends tell me that Ancestry.com is hands-down the best place because of the power and convenience of its indexes and search tools. It does sound matches for names and wildcard searches and once you realize that the spelling of an individual or a family name can change dramatically over time, you'll understand that these kinds of searches are very important. As Johni Cerny told me, if you can't find someone at Ancestry.com, they either somehow managed to skip every census, or they never existed in the first place.

However, Ancestry.com is by no means one-stop shopping for genealogists. It's full of errors and omissions and you still have to go check what you learn there against the original records. It's just a good place to start, that's all. It is also expensive. The site charges a subscription fee that is not cheap. So if you are on a budget, I'd suggest that you start your document search instead with the Church of Jesus Christ of Latter Day Saints. You don't have to go to Salt Lake City like I did; the church has what are called Family History Centers worldwide. You can go to any of these centers and order the microfilms you need and keep them as long as you have a use for them. They also have an excellent website, familysearch.org.

You should be warned, however, that the Family History Centers are not nearly as easy to use as Ancestry.com. They may contain more records, but the records are available to you on microfilm, and organized state by state, county by county, private collection by private collection. There is no central indexing. It is the largest source of genealogical data in the world—there is nothing comparable—and it's constantly expanding, but you need to know what you want to find before you start looking around or else you will waste an incredible amount of time. So before you go to one of these centers, figure out all the variant spellings of your ancestors' names and where your ancestors lived. Then, when you get to the center, there is a computerized catalog, which you generally search by place name. So you'll type in "Montgomery," for example, and it will give you a whole list of places that have the word *Montgomery* in their jurisdiction—and then it will give you a list of all the types of records—court documents, land deeds, census data, etc.—from that jurisdiction. Then you can request microfilm of each record, put it on a reader, and scan through it for your ancestor's name. There is no indexing by name (although some records may themselves contain indexes). Of course, just like Ancestry.com, the Family History Centers are by no means exhaustive.

You may also find important documents in the Freedmen's Bureau records (part of the National Archives and available online at www.archives.gov), as well as at many historical societies, public and university libraries, and newspaper archives around the country and online. The specific demands of your own search will guide you. There are a number of excellent reference books that can also help. As Jane Ailes says: "The most important issue for anyone doing genealogy research is to understand the techniques of research and to be diligent about sources, organization of data, and accurate interpretation of the documents they find."

According to Ailes, the best sources for learning these techniques are the following:

Henry Campbell Black. *Black's Law Dictionary.* 1st edition 1891 and 2nd edition 1910. (CDROM edition of the two editions of the dictionary, Archive CD Books USA, ISBN 1-933828-08-0.)

Joan F. Curran, Madilyn C. Crane, and John H. Wray. *Numbering Your Genealogy: Basic Systems, Complex Families, and International Kin.* Arlington, Virginia: National Genealogical Society, 2000.

William Dollarhide. *The Census Book: A Genealogist's Guide to Federal Census Facts, Schedules and Indexes.* North Salt Lake, Utah: Heritage Quest, 2000.

Colleen Fitzpatrick and Andrew Yeiser. *DNA & Genealogy.* Fountain Valley, California: Rice Book Press, 2005.

Val D. Greenwood. *The Researcher's Guide to American Genealogy, 3rd edition.* Baltimore: Genealogical Publishing Co., 2000.

E. Wade Hone. *Land & Property Research in the United States.* Salt Lake City: Ancestry, Inc., 1997.

Elizabeth S. Mills. *Evidence: Citation & Analysis for the Family Historian.* Baltimore: Genealogical Publishing Co., 1997.

Elizabeth S. Mills, editor. *Professional Genealogy: A Manual for Researchers, Writers, Editors, Lecturers, and Librarians.* Baltimore: Genealogical Publishing Co., 2001.

Elizabeth S. Mills. *Evidence Explained: Citing History Sources from Artifacts to Cyberspace.* Baltimore: Genealogical Publishing Co., 2007.

James C. Neagles. *U.S. Military Records: A Guide to Federal and State Sources, Colonial America to the Present.* Orem, Utah: Ancestry Publishing, an imprint of MyFamily.com, Inc., 1994.

Christine Rose. *Genealogical Proof Standard: Building a Solid Case.* San Jose, California: CR Publications, 2005.

Loretto D. Szucs and Sandra H. Luebking, editors. *The Source: A Guidebook to American Genealogy, 3rd edition.* Provo, Utah: Ancestry Publishing, a division of MyFamily.com, Inc., 2006.

William Thorndale and William Dollarhide. *Map Guide to the U.S. Federal Censuses, 1790–1920.* Baltimore: Genealogical Publishing Co., 1987.

You can also find articles in the journal of the National Genealogical Society, the *National Genealogical Society Quarterly,* which covers a myriad of topics related to genealogical research, including

African American research. These articles are juried and go through an editorial process, so they are of good quality. The journal is usually available at any library that has a section on genealogy.

Remember that African Americans face unique problems in researching their family trees. The fact that the vast majority of our ancestors were slaves until 1865 means that no census prior to 1870 is going to contain their names. So black Americans who are trying to trace their families back past 1870 must try to find the name of their last enslaved ancestor's owner prior to emancipation. These can be found in the slave schedules that were part of the census in 1850 and 1860 and in the estate records of the Old South. But that search will often prove fruitless, and even under the best circumstances, you will have great difficulty tracing your family into the slave period. There are many excellent books and articles on this subject. As a start, I'd recommend the following few for anyone researching African American families:

Curtis G. Brasfield. "Tracing Slave Ancestors: Batchelor, Bradley, Branch, and Wright of Desha County, Arkansas," *National Genealogical Society Quarterly* 92, no. 1 (March 2004), pp. 6–30.

James F. Brooks, editor. *Confounding the Color Line: The Indian-Black Experience in North America.* Lincoln and London: University of Nebraska Press, 2002.

Tony Burroughs. *Black Roots: A Beginner's Guide to Tracing the African American Family Tree.* New York: Fireside Books, 2001.

Virginia E. DeMarce. "Looking at Legends—Lumbee and Melungeon: Applied Genealogy and the Origins of Tri-racial Isolate Settlements," *National Genealogical Society Quarterly* 81, no. 1 (March 1993), pp. 24–45.

Virginia E. DeMarce. "Review Essay: *The Melungeons,*" *National Genealogical Society Quarterly* 84, no. 2 (June 1996), pp. 135–49.

182 · Resources for Building Your Family Tree

Virginia E. DeMarce. " 'Verry Slitly Mixt': Tri-Racial Isolate Families of the Upper South—A Genealogical Study," *National Genealogical Society Quarterly* 80, no. 1 (March 1992), pp. 5–35.

David Eltis, Stephen D. Behrendt, David Richardson and Herbert S. Klein. *The Transatlantic Slave Trade: A Database on CD-ROM.* Cambridge, 1999.

David Eltis, Stephen D. Behrendt, David Richardson and Manolo Florentino, *The Transatlantic Slave Trade: An Enhanced and On-line Database* (forthcoming in 2008).

Herbert G. Gutman. *The Black Family in Slavery & Freedom, 1750–1925.* New York: Pantheon Books, 1976.

Jefferson-Hemings: A Special Issue of the National Genealogical Society Quarterly. *National Genealogical Society Quarterly* 89, no. 3 (September 2001).

Elizabeth Shown Mills. "Ethnicity and the Southern Genealogist: Myths and Misconceptions, Resources and Opportunities," Chapter Five in Robert M. Taylor, Jr., and Ralph J. Crandall, editors. *Generations and Change: Genealogical Perspectives in Social History.* Macon, Georgia: Mercer University Press, 1986, pp. 89–108.

Gary B. Mills. "Can Researchers 'Prove' the 'Unprovable'? A Selective Bibliography of Efforts to Genealogically Document Children of Master-Slave Relationships," *National Genealogical Society Quarterly* 89, no. 3 (September 2001), pp. 234–37.

Gary B. Mills. "Tracing Free People of Color in the Antebellum South: Methods, Sources, and Perspectives," *National Genealogical Society Quarterly* 78, no. 4 (December 1990), pp. 262–78.

Christopher A. Nordmann. "Jumping Over the Broomstick: Resources for Documenting Slave 'Marriages,' " *National Genealogical Society Quarterly* 91, no. 3 (September 2003), pp. 196–216.

David E. Paterson. "Georgia's Slave Population in Legal Records: Where and How to Look, an Introduction to courthouse resources," digital image, http://www.rootsweb.com/~gapike/slave.htm.

Edward T. Price. "A Geographic Analysis of White-Negro-Indian Racial Mixtures in Eastern United States," *Annals of the Association of American Geographers* 43, no. 2 (June 1953), pp. 138–55.

Dee Parmer Woodtor. *Finding a Place Called Home: A Guide to African American Genealogy and Historical Identity.* New York: Random House, 1999.

Additionally, I would recommend consulting the following websites, all of which we used in researching Oprah's family history:

Large Slaveholders of 1860 and African American Surname Matches from 1870. Tom Blake, compiler. http://freepages.genealogy.rootsweb.com/~ajac/.

List of Slaves from the 1860 census, age 100 and up. Tom Blake, compiler. http://freepages.genealogy.rootsweb.com/~ajac/slave100up.htm

Mississippi Department of Archives and History http://mdah.state.ms.us/.

North American Slave Narratives. University of North Carolina Library, Documenting the American South. http://docsouth.unc.edu/neh/.

Records of the Bureau of Refugees, Freedmen, and Abandoned Lands. Record Group 105. http://www.archives.gov/research/guide-fed-records/groups/105.html.

Researching Southern Claims Commission Records. St. Louis County Library. http://www.slcl.org/branches/hq/sc/scc/scc-main.htm.

Slave Narratives from the Federal Writers' Project, 1936–1938.

Library of Congress, American Memory. http://memory.loc.
gov/ammem/snhtml/snhome.html.

In the end, African Americans who've taken their family tree
back as far as traditional genealogical research will allow have to
decide if they want to undergo DNA testing to try to take it back
even further. There are quite a large number of companies that will
do this (Rick Kittles's African Ancestry.com is a good one). I recommend that you do it twice, with two different companies, so that
you can better evaluate the results. The tests are simple—usually
just a swab of your cheek is all they want—and the whole thing can
be done through the mail. They are not cheap, though, and the results can be inconclusive or very complicated to assess. In the end,
you will learn the names of one or more ethnic groups that share
genetic markers with you. It will then be up to you to learn as
much as you care to about those groups—which will almost invariably involve studying the history of Africa and of the trans-Atlantic
slave trade. There are innumerable excellent books on this subject.
I'd recommend the following as a start:

John W. Blassingame. *The Slave Community.* New York: Oxford Uni-
    versity Press, 1972.
Sylviane A. Diouf, editor. *Fighting the Slave Trade: West African Strate-
    gies.* Athens: Ohio University Press, 2003.
David Eltis. *The Rise of African Slavery in the Americas.* New York:
    Cambridge University Press, 1999.
Michael Angelo Gomez. *Exchanging Our Country Marks: The Transfor-
    mation of African Identities in the Colonial and Ante-Bellum South.*
    Chapel Hill: University of North Carolina Press, 1998.
Walter Hawthorne. *Planting Rice and Harvesting Slaves: Transformations
    along the Guinea-Bissau Coast, 1450–1850.* Portsmouth, New
    Hampshire: Heinemann, 2003.

Linda Heywood, editor. *Central Africans and Cultural Transformations in the American Diaspora.* New York: Cambridge University Press, 2000.

Linda Heywood and John Thornton. *Central Africans, Atlantic Creoles and the Making of the Anglo-Dutch Americas.* New York: Cambridge University Press, 2007.

Adam Jones. *From Slaves to Palm Kernels: A History of the Galhinas Country (West Africa) 1730–1890.* Wiesbaden: F. Steiner, 1983.

James A. McMillin. *The Final Victims: Foreign Slave Trade to North America, 1783–1810.* Columbia: University of South Carolina Press, 2004.

Joseph Miller. *Way of Death: Merchant Capitalism and the Angolan Slave Trade, 1730–1830.* Madison: University of Wisconsin Press, 1988.

Walter Rodney. *History of the Upper Guinea Coast, 1545–1800.* Oxford: Clarendon Press, 1970 (reprint, New York: Monthly Review Press, 1980).

Robert B. Shaw. *A Legal History of Slavery in the United States.* Potsdam, New York: Northern Press, 1991.

John Thornton. *Africa and Africans in the Making of the Atlantic World 1400–1800.* New York: Cambridge University Press, 1998.

John Thornton. *Warfare in Atlantic Africa, 1500–1800.* London: Routledge, 1998.

So that's it. I don't know if this brief overview has made you any more confident about researching your own family tree. I hope it has, though, because in my experience there are few thing more rewarding than knowing where you came from.

Acknowledgments

I would like to thank the following people for their generous assistance: Angela De Leon, Sabin Streeter, Jane Ailes, Bennett Ashley, Tina Bennett, Ira Berlin, Anne Brown, Vincent Brown, Tony Burroughs, Rudolph Byrd, Johni Cerny, Jill Cowan, Barbara Delutis, David Eltis, Liza Gates, Maggie Gates, Asako Gladsjo, Robert Gold, Linda Heywood, Evelyn Brooks Higginbotham, Jan Hillegas, Rick Horgan, Glenn Hutchins, Graham Judd, Erin Kasimow, Joanne Kendall, Peter Kunhardt, Bill Lamar, Julia Marchesi, Michael Maron, Dyllan McGee, Angelique McFarland, Michelle McIntyre, Lynn Nesbit, Chris Nordmann, Susan O'Donovan, Amilca Palmer, Julian Pavia, DaVida Rice, Tammy Robinson, Leslie Rowland, Ingrid Saunders-Jones, John Sexton, Hanne Small, John Thornton, Kelly Wheeler, Indra Wilson, Abby Wolf, Donald Yacovonne.

I would also like to thank the Coca-Cola Company and the McDonald's Corporation for their sponsorship of *Oprah's Roots* and *African American Lives II,* especially Ingrid Saunders-Jones and William Lamar.

Index

Note: **Boldfaced** references indicate photographs.

Kpelle people, 155, 158, 160–62,
163–64
Ku Klux Klan, 73, 76–77

L

land deeds, 82, 99, 177
land ownership, 134–40, 167
Lee, Earlist (grandfather), 46, 65
Lee, Elizabeth (great-
grandmother), 118–19
Lee, Grace (great-great-
grandmother), 119
Lee, Harold (great-grandfather),
118–19
Lee, John (great-great-
grandfather), 119
Lee, S.E., 119, 120
Lee, Vernita (mother), 43, 44, 46,
48–50, **49**
libraries, 81, 179

M

Mallet, Luther, 75, 76–78
marriage, between slaves, 104
marriage licenses, 99
marriage records, 37, 177
matrilineal ancestry, 154–55
military records, 177
Mills, Elizabeth Shown, 107–8
Morrison, Toni, 168

N

National Archives, 81, 114
National Genealogical Society,
180–81
*National Genealogical Society
Quarterly,* 180–81

Native Americans, 32, 152–53
newspapers, 177, 179

O

obituaries, 177
Oldendorp, Georg, 160
Oprah's Roots (PBS documentary),
24–25
oral history
importance of, 33–34, 37–38,
93
interview process, 36–37,
176–77
methodology, 30–31
self-censorship trends in,
34–35
validating stories from, 31–32,
33–34, 36–37

P

PBS documentary films, 23–25,
27
A Peculiar People (Creel), 159
Presley, Hattie Mae (grandmother), 44, 46, **47**, 48, 54,
65–66, 69, 88
Presley, Nelson Alexander
(great-grandfather), 84, 87
property ownership, 134–40, 167

R

racism, internalization of, 50–51,
149, 168
Reconstruction Era, 96, 114, 132
Rinaldi, Matthew, 75–76, 77–78
Rosenwald, Julius, 84
Rowland, Leslie, 95, 116, 117

Mississippi
COUNTY Montgomery
TOWNSHIP OR OTHER DIVISION OF COUNTY — Beat 5 — Parish
NAME OF INCORPOR
NAME OF INSTITUTION

LOCATION			NAME	RELATION	PERSONAL DESCRIPTION						NATIVITY	
											Place of birth of this Person	Place of birth of Father
			Russell Mary J.	Head		W	Wd	63	Wd	8	Mississippi	Alabama
			Willie J.	Son	M	B	21	S			Mississippi	Mississippi
			John N.	Son	M	B	23	S			Mississippi	Mississippi
			Ola M.	Daughter		W		S			Mississippi	Mississippi
			Ernest	Son	M	B	12	S			Mississippi	Mississippi
			William	Son	M	B	8	S			Mississippi	Mississippi
			Emma	Daughter		B	9	S			Mississippi	Mississippi
			Brees Russell	Head Son	M	B	13	S			Mississippi	Mississippi
			Mitchell Jesse	Head	M	B	40	M1	22		Mississippi	United States
			Maggie E.	Wife		B	39	M1	7	7	Mississippi	Georgia
			Arthur N.	Son	M	B	18	S			Mississippi	Mississippi
			Pearl A.	Daughter		B	15	S			Mississippi	Mississippi
			Sam	Daughter		B	13	S			Mississippi	Mississippi
			Zora M.	Daughter		B	10	S			Mississippi	Mississippi
			Jessie A.	Daughter		B	8	S			Mississippi	Mississippi
			Early C.	Daughter		B	6	S			Mississippi	Mississippi
			Solomon J.	Son	M	B	12	S			Mississippi	Mississippi
			Jones Stella	Boarder		B	3	S			Mississippi	Mississippi
			Murray Constantine	Head	M	B	70	M1	33		Georgia	Georgia
			Violet J.	Wife		B	71	M1	33	7 7	North Carolina	North Carolina
			Murray Gladys M.	Head		B	39	M5		8 8	Mississippi	Georgia
			Aus. M.	Son	M	B	8				Mississippi	Mississippi
			Anna J.	Daughter		B	10				Mississippi	Mississippi
			Ida J.	Daughter		B	16				Mississippi	Mississippi
			James N.	Son	M	B	12				Mississippi	Mississippi
			Ada J.	Daughter		B	5				Mississippi	Mississippi
			Murray Sanford	Head	M	B	38	M1	14		Mississippi	Georgia
			Ella	Wife		B	36	M1	14	7 7	Mississippi	Georgia
			Andre	Son	M	B	13	S			Mississippi	Mississippi
			Morris	Son	M	B	10	S			Mississippi	Mississippi
			Clara	Son		B	7	S			Mississippi	Mississippi
			Nellie	Son	M	B	5	S			Mississippi	Mississippi
			Russell C.	Son	M	B	3	S			Mississippi	Mississippi
			Henry	Daughter		B	12	S			Mississippi	Mississippi
			Ira	Daughter		B	12	S			Mississippi	Mississippi
			Robertson Pope J.	Head	M	W	30	M1	7		Mississippi	South Carolina
			Julia J.	Wife		W	30	M1	7	4 3	Mississippi	Mississippi
			Edna M.	Daughter		W	5	S			Mississippi	Mississippi
			Lloyd L.	Son	M	W	3	S			Mississippi	Mississippi
			Luther W.	Son	M	W	6/12	S			Mississippi	Mississippi
			Henry C.	Father	M	W	60	M1	33		South Carolina	Tennessee
			Ellen J.	Mother		W	60	M2	41	4 3	Mississippi	Georgia
			Aaton Joseph J.	Head	M	W	20	M1	2		Mississippi	South Carolina
			Mand E.	Wife		W	16	M1	2	2 2	Mississippi	Mississippi
			Selina M.	Daughter		W	1	S			Mississippi	Mississippi
			Selma	Daughter		W	1/12	S			Mississippi	Mississippi
			Palmertree John	Head	M	W	34	M1	10		Mississippi	Mississippi
			Mary L.	Wife		W	24	M1	10	4 4	Mississippi	Mississippi
			William R.	Son	M	W	10	S			Mississippi	Mississippi